99 *crochet* Post Stitches

WOW! Ninety-nine tempting textures to crochet!

Your favorite hobby comes alive with real depth and richness in Darla Sims's latest collection of exciting pattern stitches. Post Stitches are the simple magic giving these patterns their extra pizzazz! Choose from pattern stitches worked closely for warmth or others yielding a light and lacy look. You can make afghans, scarves, shawls, table runners—anything your creative spirit desires—with these lovely and touchable Post Stitch patterns.

Visit your local retailer or www.leisurearts.com to complete your Leisure Arts pattern library with these leaflets:

Meet Darla Sims

"When I did my first collection of 63 crochet stitches," says Darla Sims, "I thought I'd never do it again. Yet when it was completed, I discovered I'd developed a fascination with finding and creating new stitches."

The Washington state native lives outside of Seattle and enjoys spending time with her grown children, grandkids, and great-grandchildren.

Darla is also a regular contributor to a crochet magazine.

"I write articles about the technical side of crochet," she explains.

"In the past," Darla says, "I did some work with knitting, but these days I design crochet exclusively. For some of my crochet pattern stitches, I'm able to get a look similar to knitting. It's a matter of thinking differently about where to place the hook while crocheting. You can create the seemingly impossible when you keep looking at things in different ways."

LEISURE ARTS, INC.
Little Rock, Arkansas

Receding Shells

Chain a multiple of 11 + 2 chs.

Row 1 (Right side)**:** Dc in fourth ch from hook (**3 skipped chs count as first dc**), skip next 2 chs, 3 dc in next ch, dc in next ch, 3 dc in next ch, ★ skip next 2 chs, dc in next 4 chs, skip next 2 chs, 3 dc in next ch, dc in next ch, 3 dc in next ch; repeat from ★ across to last 4 chs, skip next 2 chs, dc in last 2 chs.

Note: Loop a short piece of yarn around any stitch to mark Row 1 as **right** side.

To work Back Post double crochet (abbreviated BPdc), YO, insert hook from **back** to **front** around post of dc indicated *(Fig. 1, page 79)*, YO and pull up a loop (3 loops on hook), (YO and draw through 2 loops on hook) twice.

Row 2: Ch 3 (**counts as first dc, now and throughout**), turn; dc in next dc, ch 2, skip next 2 dc, work BPdc around next dc, dc in next dc, work BPdc around next dc, ch 2, ★ skip next 2 dc, dc in next 4 dc, ch 2, skip next 2 dc, work BPdc around next dc, dc in next dc, work BPdc around next dc, ch 2; repeat from ★ across to last 4 dc, skip next 2 dc, dc in last 2 dc.

Row 3: Ch 3, turn; dc in next dc, 3 dc in next BPdc, dc in next dc, 3 dc in next BPdc, ★ dc in next 4 dc, 3 dc in next BPdc, dc in next dc, 3 dc in next BPdc; repeat from ★ across to last 2 dc, dc in last 2 dc.

Repeat Rows 2 and 3 for pattern.

Ladders

Chain a multiple of 8 chs.

Row 1 (Right side)**:** Dc in fourth ch from hook (**3 skipped chs count as first dc**) and in each ch across.

Note: Loop a short piece of yarn around any stitch to mark Row 1 as **right** side.

To work Front Post double crochet (abbreviated FPdc), YO, insert hook from **front** to **back** around post of st indicated *(Fig. 1, page 79)*, YO and pull up a loop (3 loops on hook), (YO and draw through 2 loops on hook) twice.

To work Back Post double crochet (abbreviated BPdc), YO, insert hook from **back** to **front** around post of st indicated *(Fig. 1, page 79)*, YO and pull up a loop (3 loops on hook), (YO and draw through 2 loops on hook) twice.

Row 2: Ch 3 (**counts as first dc, now and throughout**), turn; work FPdc around each of next 4 sts, ★ work BPdc around each of next 4 sts, work FPdc around each of next 4 sts; repeat from ★ across to last dc, dc in last dc.

Row 3: Ch 3, turn; work BPdc around each of next 4 sts, ★ work FPdc around each of next 4 sts, work BPdc around each of next 4 sts; repeat from ★ across to last dc, dc in last dc.

Repeat Rows 2 and 3 for pattern.

Duet

Chain a multiple of 10 + 3 chs.

Row 1 (Right side)**:** Dc in fourth ch from hook (**3 skipped chs count as first dc**) and in next ch, ch 3, skip next ch, sc in next ch, 5 dc in next ch, sc in next ch, ch 3, ★ skip next ch, dc in next 5 chs, ch 3, skip next ch, sc in next ch, 5 dc in next ch, sc in next ch, ch 3; repeat from ★ across to last 4 chs, skip next ch, dc in last 3 chs.

Note: Loop a short piece of yarn around any stitch to mark Row 1 as **right** side.

To work Back Post double crochet (abbreviated BPdc), YO, insert hook from **back** to **front** around post of dc indicated (**Fig. 1, page 79**), YO and pull up a loop (3 loops on hook), (YO and draw through 2 loops on hook) twice.

Row 2: Ch 3 (**counts as first dc, now and throughout**), turn; work BPdc around each of next 2 dc, ch 3, skip next sc and next 2 dc, sc in next dc, ch 3, ★ skip next 2 dc and next sc, work BPdc around each of next 5 dc, ch 3, skip next sc and next 2 dc, sc in next dc, ch 3; repeat from ★ across to last 6 sts, skip next 2 dc and next sc, work BPdc around each of next 2 dc, dc in last dc.

Row 3: Ch 3, turn; dc in next 2 BPdc, ch 3, sc in next ch-3 sp, 5 dc in next sc, sc in next ch-3 sp, ch 3, ★ dc in next 5 BPdc, ch 3, sc in next ch-3 sp, 5 dc in next sc, sc in next ch-3 sp, ch 3; repeat from ★ across to last 3 sts, dc in last 3 sts.

Repeat Rows 2 and 3 for pattern.

Little Boxes

Chain a multiple of 4 + 5 chs.

Row 1 (Right side)**:** Dc in fourth ch from hook (**3 skipped chs count as first dc**) and in each ch across.

Note: Loop a short piece of yarn around any stitch to mark Row 1 as **right** side.

To work Front Post double crochet (abbreviated FPdc), YO, insert hook from **front** to **back** around post of st indicated (**Fig. 1, page 79**), YO and pull up a loop (3 loops on hook), (YO and draw through 2 loops on hook) twice.

To work Back Post double crochet (abbreviated BPdc), YO, insert hook from **back** to **front** around post of st indicated (**Fig. 1, page 79**), YO and pull up a loop (3 loops on hook), (YO and draw through 2 loops on hook) twice.

Row 2: Ch 2 (**counts as first hdc**), turn; work FPdc around each of next 2 dc, work BPdc around next st, (work FPdc around each of next 3 dc, work BPdc around next st) across to last 3 dc, work FPdc around each of next 2 dc, hdc in last dc.

Row 3: Ch 3 (**counts as first dc**), turn; dc in next 2 FPdc, work FPdc around next BPdc, (dc in next 3 FPdc, work FPdc around next BPdc) across to last 3 sts, dc in last 3 sts.

Repeat Rows 2 and 3 for pattern.

Posted Chevrons

Chain a multiple of 10 + 4 chs.

Row 1 (Right side)**:** Hdc in third ch from hook (**2 skipped chs count as first hdc**) and in each ch across.

Note: Loop a short piece of yarn around any stitch to mark Row 1 as **right** side.

Row 2: Ch 2 (**counts as first hdc, now and throughout**), turn; hdc in next hdc and in each hdc across.

To work Front Post double crochet (*abbreviated FPdc*), YO, working in **front** of previous row (*Fig. 2, page 80*), insert hook from **front** to **back** around post of st indicated (*Fig. 1, page 79*), YO and pull up a loop (3 loops on hook), (YO and draw through 2 loops on hook) twice. Skip hdc behind FPdc.

Row 3: Ch 2, turn; hdc in next 5 hdc, work FPdc around hdc one row **below** next hdc, ★ hdc in next 9 hdc, work FPdc around hdc one row **below** next hdc; repeat from ★ across to last 6 hdc, hdc in last 6 hdc.

Row 4: Ch 2, turn; hdc in next st and in each st across.

Row 5: Ch 2, turn; hdc in next 4 hdc, work FPdc around st one row **below** each of next 3 hdc, ★ hdc in next 7 hdc, work FPdc around st one row **below** each of next 3 hdc; repeat from ★ across to last 5 hdc, hdc in last 5 hdc.

Row 6: Ch 2, turn; hdc in next st and in each st across.

Row 7: Ch 2, turn; hdc in next 3 hdc, work FPdc around st one row **below** each of next 5 hdc, ★ hdc in next 5 hdc, work FPdc around st one row **below** each of next 5 hdc; repeat from ★ across to last 4 hdc, hdc in last 4 hdc.

Row 8: Ch 2, turn; hdc in next st and in each st across.

Row 9: Ch 2, turn; hdc in next 2 hdc, ★ work FPdc around st one row **below** each of next 3 hdc, hdc in next hdc, work FPdc around st one row **below** each of next 3 hdc, hdc in next 3 hdc; repeat from ★ across.

Row 10: Ch 2, turn; hdc in next st and in each st across.

Row 11: Ch 2, turn; ★ hdc in next hdc, work FPdc around st one row **below** each of next 3 hdc, hdc in next 3 hdc, work FPdc around st one row **below** each of next 3 hdc; repeat from ★ across to last 2 hdc, hdc in last 2 hdc.

Row 12: Ch 2, turn; hdc in next st and in each st across.

Row 13: Ch 2, turn; work FPdc around st one row **below** each of next 3 hdc, hdc in next 5 hdc, ★ work FPdc around st one row **below** each of next 5 hdc, hdc in next 5 hdc; repeat from ★ across to last 4 hdc, work FPdc around st one row **below** each of next 3 hdc, hdc in last hdc.

Row 14: Ch 2, turn; hdc in next st and in each st across.

Row 15: Ch 2, turn; work FPdc around FPdc one row **below** each of next 2 hdc, hdc in next 7 hdc, ★ work FPdc around FPdc one row **below** each of next 3 hdc, hdc in next 7 hdc; repeat from ★ across to last 3 hdc, work FPdc around FPdc one row **below** each of next 2 hdc, hdc in last hdc.

Row 16: Ch 2, turn; hdc in next st and in each st across.

Row 17: Ch 2, turn; work FPdc around FPdc one row **below** next hdc, (hdc in next 4 hdc, work FPdc around st one row **below** next hdc) across to last hdc, hdc in last hdc.

Repeat Rows 4-17 for pattern.

Textured Diagonal

Chain a multiple of 8 + 4 chs.

Row 1 (Right side): Dc in fourth ch from hook (**3 skipped chs count as first dc**) and in each ch across.

Note: Loop a short piece of yarn around any stitch to mark Row 1 as **right** side.

To work Front Post double crochet (abbreviated FPdc), YO, insert hook from **front** to **back** around post of st indicated (**Fig. 1, page 79**), YO and pull up a loop (3 loops on hook), (YO and draw through 2 loops on hook) twice.

To work Back Post double crochet (abbreviated BPdc), YO, insert hook from **back** to **front** around post of st indicated (**Fig. 1, page 79**), YO and pull up a loop (3 loops on hook), (YO and draw through 2 loops on hook) twice.

Row 2: Ch 2 (**counts as first hdc, now and throughout**), turn; ★ work FPdc around each of next 4 dc, work BPdc around each of next 4 dc; repeat from ★ across to last dc, hdc in last dc.

Row 3: Ch 2, turn; work FPdc around each of next 3 sts, work BPdc around each of next 4 sts, ★ work FPdc around each of next 4 sts, work BPdc around each of next 4 sts; repeat from ★ across to last 2 sts, work FPdc around next st, hdc in last hdc.

Row 4: Ch 2, turn; work BPdc around each of next 2 sts, work FPdc around each of next 4 sts, ★ work BPdc around each of next 4 sts, work FPdc around each of next 4 sts; repeat from ★ across to last 3 sts, work BPdc around each of next 2 sts, hdc in last hdc.

Row 5: Ch 2, turn; work FPdc around next st, work BPdc around each of next 4 sts, ★ work FPdc around each of next 4 sts, work BPdc around each of next 4 sts; repeat from ★ across to last 4 sts, work FPdc around each of next 3 sts, hdc in last hdc.

Row 6: Ch 2, turn; ★ work BPdc around each of next 4 sts, work FPdc around each of next 4 sts; repeat from ★ across to last hdc, hdc in last hdc.

Row 7: Ch 2, turn; work BPdc around each of next 3 sts, work FPdc around each of next 4 sts, ★ work BPdc around each of next 4 sts, work FPdc around each of next 4 sts; repeat from ★ across to last 2 sts, work BPdc around next st, hdc in last hdc.

Row 8: Ch 2, turn; work FPdc around each of next 2 sts, work BPdc around each of next 4 sts, ★ work FPdc around each of next 4 sts, work BPdc around each of next 4 sts; repeat from ★ across to last 3 sts, work FPdc around each of next 2 sts, hdc in last hdc.

Row 9: Ch 2, turn; work BPdc around next st, work FPdc around each of next 4 sts, ★ work BPdc around each of next 4 sts, work FPdc around each of next 4 sts; repeat from ★ across to last 4 sts, work BPdc around each of next 3 sts, hdc in last hdc.

Row 10: Ch 2, turn; ★ work FPdc around each of next 4 sts, work BPdc around each of next 4 sts; repeat from ★ across to last dc, hdc in last hdc.

Repeat Rows 3-10 for pattern.

Beads on a String

Chain a multiple of 8 + 4 chs.

Row 1 (Right side): Sc in second ch from hook and in each ch across.

Note: Loop a short piece of yarn around any stitch to mark Row 1 as **right** side.

Row 2: Ch 1, turn; sc in each sc across.

To work Popcorn (uses one sc), 5 sc in sc indicated, drop loop from hook, insert hook from **front** to **back** in first sc of 5-sc group, hook dropped loop and draw through st.

To work Front Post double crochet (abbreviated FPdc), YO, working in **front** of previous row *(Fig. 2, page 80)*, insert hook from **front** to **back** around post of st indicated *(Fig. 1, page 79)*, YO and pull up a loop (3 loops on hook), (YO and draw through 2 loops on hook) twice. Skip sc behind FPdc.

Row 3: Ch 1, turn; sc in first sc, work Popcorn in next sc, ★ sc in next 3 sc, work FPdc around st one row **below** next sc, sc in next 3 sc, work Popcorn in next sc; repeat from ★ across to last sc, sc in last sc.

Row 4: Ch 1, turn; sc in each st across.

Rows 5-8: Repeat Rows 3 and 4 twice.

Row 9: Ch 1, turn; sc in first sc, work FPdc around st one row **below** next sc, ★ sc in next 3 sc, work Popcorn in next sc, sc in next 3 sc, work FPdc around st one row **below** next sc; repeat from ★ across to last sc, sc in last sc.

Row 10: Ch 1, turn; sc in each st across.

Rows 11-14: Repeat Rows 9 and 10 twice.

Repeat Rows 3-14 for pattern.

Angel Wings

Note: Uses MC and CC in the following sequence: ★ One row **each** MC, CC; repeat from ★ for stripe sequence.

With MC, chain a multiple of 8 + 4 chs.

Row 1 (Wrong side): Dc in fourth ch from hook (**3 skipped chs count as first dc**) and in each ch across; finish off.

Note: Loop a short piece of yarn around the **back** of any stitch on Row 1 to mark **right** side.

To work Front Post treble crochet *(abbreviated FPtr)*, YO twice, insert hook from **front** to **back** around post of dc indicated *(Fig. 1, page 79)*, YO and pull up a loop (4 loops on hook), (YO and draw through 2 loops on hook) 3 times.

To work Front Post double treble crochet *(abbreviated FPdtr)*, YO 3 times, insert hook from **front** to **back** around post of dc indicated *(Fig. 1, page 79)*, YO and pull up a loop (5 loops on hook), (YO and draw through 2 loops on hook) 4 times.

To work Front Post triple treble crochet *(abbreviated FPtrtr)*, YO 4 times, insert hook from **front** to **back** around post of dc indicated *(Fig. 1, page 79)*, YO and pull up a loop (6 loops on hook), (YO and draw through 2 loops on hook) 5 times.

Row 2: With **right** side facing, join CC with dc in first dc *(see Joining With Dc, page 79)*; skip next 3 dc, work (FPtrtr, FPdtr, FPtr) from **bottom** to **top** around next dc, dc in same dc worked around **and** in next dc, work (FPtr, FPdtr, FPtrtr) from **top** to **bottom** around last dc worked into, ★ skip next 6 dc, work (FPtrtr, FPdtr, FPtr) from **bottom** to **top** around next dc, dc in same dc worked around **and** in next dc, work (FPtr, FPdtr, FPtrtr) from **top** to **bottom** around last dc worked into; repeat from ★ across to last 4 dc, skip next 3 dc, dc in last dc; finish off.

Row 3: With **wrong** side facing, join MC with dc in first dc; dc in next st and in each st across; finish off.

Repeat Rows 2 and 3 for pattern.

Inverted Shells

Chain a multiple of 8 + 7 chs.

To decrease *(uses next 5 chs)*, † YO, insert hook in **next** ch, YO and pull up a loop, YO and draw through 2 loops on hook †; repeat from † to † once **more**, skip next ch, repeat from † to † 2 times, YO and draw through all 5 loops on hook.

Row 1 (Right side)**:** Dc in fourth ch from hook **(3 skipped chs count as first dc)** and in next 2 chs, ch 2, decrease, ch 2, ★ dc in next 3 chs, ch 2, decrease, ch 2; repeat from ★ across to last 4 chs, dc in last 4 chs.

Note: Loop a short piece of yarn around any stitch to mark Row 1 as **right** side.

To work Front Post double crochet *(abbreviated FPdc)*, YO, insert hook from **front** to **back** around post of st indicated *(Fig. 1, page 79)*, YO and pull up a loop (3 loops on hook), (YO and draw through 2 loops on hook) twice.

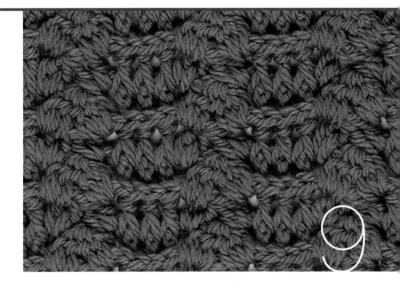

To work Cluster *(uses next 2 ch-2 sps)*, ★ YO, insert hook in **next** ch-2 sp, YO and pull up a loop, YO and draw through 2 loops on hook, YO, insert hook in **same** sp, YO and pull up a loop, YO and draw through 2 loops on hook; repeat from ★ once **more**, YO and draw through all 5 loops on hook.

Row 2: Ch 3 **(counts as first dc)**, turn; work FPdc around each of next 3 sts, ★ ch 2, work Cluster, ch 2, work FPdc around each of next 3 sts; repeat from ★ across to last dc, dc in last dc.

Repeat Row 2 for pattern.

Basket Weave

Chain a multiple of 8 + 4 chs.

Row 1 (Right side)**:** Dc in fourth ch from hook **(3 skipped chs count as first dc)** and in each ch across.

Note: Loop a short piece of yarn around any stitch to mark Row 1 as **right** side.

To work Front Post double crochet (abbreviated FPdc), YO, insert hook from **front** to **back** around post of st indicated *(Fig. 1, page 79)*, YO and pull up a loop (3 loops on hook), (YO and draw through 2 loops on hook) twice.

To work Back Post double crochet (abbreviated BPdc), YO, insert hook from **back** to **front** around post of st indicated *(Fig. 1, page 79)*, YO and pull up a loop (3 loops on hook), (YO and draw through 2 loops on hook) twice.

Rows 2 and 3: Ch 2 **(counts as first hdc, now and throughout)**, turn; ★ work FPdc around each of next 4 sts, work BPdc around each of next 4 sts; repeat from ★ across to last st, hdc in last st.

Rows 4 and 5: Ch 2, turn; ★ work BPdc around each of next 4 sts, work FPdc around each of next 4 sts; repeat from ★ across to last st, hdc in last st.

Repeat Rows 2-5 for pattern.

Sculpted Shells

Chain a multiple of 11 + 15 chs.

To treble crochet (abbreviated tr), YO twice, insert hook in st or sp indicated, YO and pull up a loop (4 loops on hook), (YO and draw through 2 loops on hook) 3 times.

Row 1 (Right side)**:** Tr in fifth ch from hook **(4 skipped chs count as first tr)** and in next ch, dc in next 2 chs, hdc in next 2 chs, dc in next 2 chs, ★ tr in next 2 chs, ch 1, skip next ch, tr in next 2 chs, dc in next 2 chs, hdc in next 2 chs, dc in next 2 chs; repeat from ★ across to last 3 chs, tr in last 3 chs.

Note: Loop a short piece of yarn around any stitch to mark Row 1 as **right** side.

To work Front Post double crochet 10 together (abbreviated FPdc10tog) (uses next 10 sts), ★ YO, insert hook from **front** to **back** around post of **next** st *(Fig. 1, page 79)*, YO and pull up a loop, YO and draw through 2 loops on hook; repeat from ★ 9 times **more**, YO and draw through all 11 loops on hook.

Row 2: Ch 1, turn; sc in first tr, ch 4, work FPdc10tog, ch 4, ★ sc in next ch-1 sp, ch 4, work FPdc10tog, ch 4; repeat from ★ across to last tr, sc in last tr.

Row 3: Ch 4 **(counts as first tr)**, turn; (2 tr, 2 dc, hdc) in next ch-4 sp, (hdc, 2 dc, 2 tr) in next ch-4 sp, ★ ch 1, (2 tr, 2 dc, hdc) in next ch-4 sp, (hdc, 2 dc, 2 tr) in next ch-4 sp; repeat from ★ across to last sc, tr in last sc.

Repeat Rows 2 and 3 for pattern.

Odessey

Chain a multiple of 6 + 3 chs.

Row 1 (Wrong side)**:** Dc in fourth ch from hook **(3 skipped chs count as first dc)**, ch 3, ★ skip next 3 chs, dc in next 3 chs, ch 3; repeat from ★ across to last 5 chs, skip next 3 chs, dc in last 2 chs.

Note: Loop a short piece of yarn around the **back** of any stitch on Row 1 to mark **right** side.

To work Split Front Post double crochet (abbreviated Split FPdc) (uses next 2 dc), ★ YO, insert hook from **front** to **back** around post of **next** dc *(Fig. 1, page 79)*, YO and pull up a loop, YO and draw through 2 loops on hook; repeat from ★ once **more**, YO and draw through all 3 loops on hook.

Row 2: Ch 5 **(counts as first dc plus ch 2)**, turn; work Split FPdc, ch 2, dc in next dc, ★ ch 2, work Split FPdc, ch 2, dc in next dc; repeat from ★ across.

Row 3: Ch 3 **(counts as first dc, now and throughout)**, turn; ★ dc in next ch-2 sp, ch 3, dc in next ch-2 sp and in next dc; repeat from ★ across.

Row 4: Ch 1, turn; sc in first 2 dc, ch 3, (sc in next 3 dc, ch 3) across to last 2 dc, sc in last 2 dc.

Row 5: Ch 3, turn; dc in next sc, ch 3, (dc in next 3 sc, ch 3) across to last 2 sc, dc in last 2 sc.

Repeat Rows 2-5 for pattern.

Gull Stitch

Chain a multiple of 6 + 3 chs.

Row 1 (Right side)**:** Dc in fourth ch from hook **(3 skipped chs count as first dc)** and in next 4 chs, ch 1, ★ skip next ch, dc in next 5 chs, ch 1; repeat from ★ across to last 7 chs, skip next ch, dc in last 6 chs.

Note: Loop a short piece of yarn around any stitch to mark Row 1 as **right** side.

Row 2: Ch 1, turn; sc in each dc and in each ch-1 sp across.

To work Front Post treble crochet (abbreviated FPtr), YO twice, working in **front** of previous row *(Fig. 2, page 80)*, insert hook from **front** to **back** around post of dc indicated *(Fig. 1, page 79)*, YO and pull up a loop (4 loops on hook), (YO and draw through 2 loops on hook) 3 times.

Row 3: Ch 3 **(counts as first dc)**, turn; skip next 2 sc, work FPtr around dc one row **below** next sc, skip next sc from first dc made, dc in next 3 sc, work FPtr around same dc as first FPtr made, ★ ch 1, skip next 4 sc from last dc made, work FPtr around dc one row **below** next sc, skip next 3 sc from last dc made, dc in next 3 sc, work FPtr around same dc as last FPtr made; repeat from ★ across to last 2 sc, skip next sc from last dc made, dc in last sc.

Row 4: Ch 1, turn; sc in each st and in each ch-1 sp across.

Repeat Rows 3 and 4 for pattern.

Boxed Shells

Chain a multiple of 10 + 3 chs.

Row 1 (Wrong side): Dc in fourth ch from hook (**3 skipped chs count as first dc**) and in next dc, skip next 2 chs, (2 dc, ch 1, 2 dc) in next ch, ★ skip next 2 chs, dc in next 5 chs, skip next 2 chs, (2 dc, ch 1, 2 dc) in next ch; repeat from ★ across to last 5 chs, skip next 2 chs, dc in last 3 chs.

Note: Loop a short piece of yarn around the **back** of any stitch on Row 1 to mark **right** side.

To work Front Post double crochet (abbreviated FPdc), YO, insert hook from **front** to **back** around post of st indicated (**Fig. 1, page 79**), YO and pull up a loop (3 loops on hook), (YO and draw through 2 loops on hook) twice.

Row 2: Ch 3 (**counts as first dc, now and throughout**), turn; work FPdc around each of next 2 dc, (2 dc, ch 1, 2 dc) in next ch-1 sp, ★ skip next 2 dc, work FPdc around each of next 5 dc, (2 dc, ch 1, 2 dc) in next ch-1 sp; repeat from ★ across to last 5 dc, skip next 2 dc, work FPdc around each of next 2 dc, dc in last dc.

To work Back Post double crochet (abbreviated BPdc), YO, insert hook from **back** to **front** around post of st indicated (**Fig. 1, page 79**), YO and pull up a loop (3 loops on hook), (YO and draw through 2 loops on hook) twice.

Row 3: Ch 3, turn; work BPdc around each of next 2 FPdc, (2 dc, ch 1, 2 dc) in next ch-1 sp, ★ skip next 2 dc, work BPdc around each of next 5 FPdc, (2 dc, ch 1, 2 dc) in next ch-1 sp; repeat from ★ across to last 5 sts, skip next 2 dc, work BPdc around each of next 2 FPdc, dc in last dc.

Row 4: Ch 3, turn; 2 dc in first dc, skip next 2 BPdc, dc in next 2 dc and in next ch-1 sp, dc in next 2 dc, ★ skip next 2 BPdc, (2 dc, ch 1, 2 dc) in next BPdc, skip next 2 BPdc, dc in next 2 dc and in next ch-1 sp, dc in next 2 dc; repeat from ★ across to last 3 sts, skip next 2 BPdc, 3 dc in last dc.

Row 5: Ch 3, turn; 2 dc in first dc, skip next 2 dc, work BPdc around each of next 5 dc, ★ (2 dc, ch 1, 2 dc) in next ch-1 sp, skip next 2 dc, work BPdc around each of next 5 dc; repeat from ★ across to last 3 dc, skip next 2 dc, 3 dc in last dc.

Row 6: Ch 3, turn; 2 dc in first dc, skip next 2 dc, work FPdc around each of next 5 BPdc, ★ (2 dc, ch 1, 2 dc) in next ch-1 sp, skip next 2 dc, work FPdc around each of next 5 BPdc; repeat from ★ across to last 3 dc, skip next 2 dc, 3 dc in last dc.

Row 7: Ch 3, turn; dc in next 2 dc, skip next 2 FPdc, (2 dc, ch 1, 2 dc) in next FPdc, ★ skip next 2 FPdc, dc in next 2 dc and in next ch-1 sp, dc in next 2 dc, skip next 2 FPdc, (2 dc, ch 1, 2 dc) in next FPdc; repeat from ★ across to last 5 sts, skip next 2 FPdc, dc in last 3 dc.

Row 8: Ch 3, turn; work FPdc around each of next 2 dc, (2 dc, ch 1, 2 dc) in next ch-1 sp, ★ skip next 2 dc, work FPdc around each of next 5 dc, (2 dc, ch 1, 2 dc) in next ch-1 sp; repeat from ★ across to last 5 dc, skip next 2 dc, work FPdc around each of next 2 dc, dc in last dc.

Repeat Rows 3-8 for pattern.

Ladders & Shells

Chain a multiple of 8 + 4 chs.

Row 1 (Right side)**:** 2 Dc in fourth ch from hook **(3 skipped chs count as first dc)**, skip next 3 chs, (dc, ch 1, dc) in next ch, ★ skip next 3 chs, (2 dc, ch 1, 2 dc) in next ch, skip next 3 chs, (dc, ch 1, dc) in next ch; repeat from ★ across to last 4 chs, skip next 3 chs, 3 dc in last ch.

Note: Loop a short piece of yarn around any stitch to mark Row 1 as **right** side.

To work Back Post double crochet (*abbreviated BPdc*)*,* YO, insert hook from **back** to **front** around post of st indicated *(Fig. 1, page 79)*, YO and pull up a loop (3 loops on hook), (YO and draw through 2 loops on hook) twice.

Row 2: Ch 3 **(counts as first dc, now and throughout)**, turn; 2 dc in first dc, skip next 2 dc, work BPdc around next dc, ch 1, work BPdc around next dc, ★ (2 dc, ch 1, 2 dc) in next ch-1 sp, skip next 2 dc, work BPdc around next dc, ch 1, work BPdc around next dc; repeat from ★ across to last 3 dc, skip next 2 dc, 3 dc in last dc.

To work Front Post double crochet (*abbreviated FPdc*)*,* YO, insert hook from **front** to **back** around post of st indicated *(Fig. 1, page 79)*, YO and pull up a loop (3 loops on hook), (YO and draw through 2 loops on hook) twice.

Row 3: Ch 3, turn; 2 dc in first dc, skip next 2 dc, work FPdc around next BPdc, ch 1, work FPdc around next BPdc, ★ (2 dc, ch 1, 2 dc) in next ch-1 sp, skip next 2 dc, work FPdc around next BPdc, ch 1, work FPdc around next BPdc; repeat from ★ across to last 3 dc, skip next 2 dc, 3 dc in last dc.

Row 4: Ch 3, turn; dc in first dc, (2 dc, ch 1, 2 dc) in next ch-1 sp, ★ (dc, ch 1, dc) in next ch-1 sp, (2 dc, ch 1, 2 dc) in next ch-1 sp; repeat from ★ across to last 4 sts, skip next 3 sts, 2 dc in last dc.

Row 5: Ch 3, turn; dc in first dc, (2 dc, ch 1, 2 dc) in next ch-1 sp, ★ skip next 2 dc, work FPdc around next dc, ch 1, work FPdc around next dc, (2 dc, ch 1, 2 dc) in next ch-1 sp; repeat from ★ across to last 4 dc, skip next 3 dc, 2 dc in last dc.

Row 6: Ch 3, turn; dc in first dc, (2 dc, ch 1, 2 dc) in next ch-1 sp, ★ skip next 2 dc, work BPdc around next FPdc, ch 1, work BPdc around next FPdc, (2 dc, ch 1, 2 dc) in next ch-1 sp; repeat from ★ across to last 4 dc, skip next 3 dc, 2 dc in last dc.

Row 7: Ch 3, turn; 2 dc in first dc, (dc, ch 1, dc) in next ch-1 sp, ★ (2 dc, ch 1, 2 dc) in next ch-1 sp, (dc, ch 1, dc) in next ch-1 sp; repeat from ★ across to last 4 dc, skip next 3 dc, 3 dc in last dc.

Row 8: Ch 3, turn; 2 dc in first dc, skip next 2 dc, work BPdc around next dc, ch 1, work BPdc around next dc, ★ (2 dc, ch 1, 2 dc) in next ch-1 sp, skip next 2 dc, work BPdc around next dc, ch 1, work BPdc around next dc; repeat from ★ across to last 3 dc, skip next 2 dc, 3 dc in last dc.

Repeat Rows 3-8 for pattern.

Posted Shells

Note: Uses MC and CC in the following sequence: ★ 2 Rows **each** MC, CC; repeat from ★ for stripe sequence.

With MC, chain a multiple of 4 chs.

Row 1 (Right side)**:** Sc in second ch from hook and in each ch across.

Note: Loop a short piece of yarn around any stitch to mark Row 1 as **right** side.

Row 2: Ch 3 (**counts as first dc, now and throughout**), turn; dc in next sc and in each sc across; finish off.

Row 3: With **right** side facing, join CC with dc in first dc (*see Joining With Dc, page 79*); skip next 2 dc, 5 dc in next dc, (skip next 3 dc, 5 dc in next dc) across to last 3 dc, skip next 2 dc, dc in last dc.

Row 4: Ch 1, turn; sc in each dc across; finish off.

To work Front Post treble crochet (abbreviated FPtr), YO twice, working in **front** of previous rows (*Fig. 2, page 80*), insert hook from **front** to **back** around post of dc indicated (*Fig. 1, page 79*), YO and pull up a loop (4 loops on hook), (YO and draw through 2 loops on hook) 3 times.

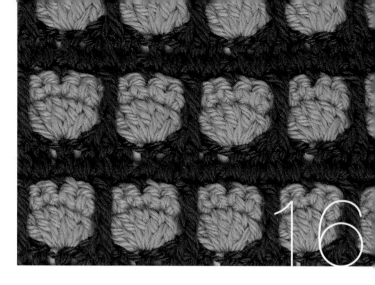

Row 5: With **right** side facing, join MC with sc in first sc (*see Joining With Sc, page 79*); work FPtr around second dc 3 rows **below**, ch 1, skip next 2 sc from last sc made, sc in next sc, ch 1, skip next 3 dc 3 rows **below**, work FPtr around next dc, ★ ch 1, skip next 4 sc from last sc made, sc in next sc, ch 1, skip next 3 dc 3 rows **below**, work FPtr around next dc; repeat from ★ across to last 3 sc, skip next 2 sc from last sc made, sc in last sc.

Row 6: Ch 3, turn; dc in next st and in each ch-1 sp and each st across; finish off.

Repeat Rows 3-6 for pattern.

Eyes Of God

Chain a multiple of 7 + 6 chs.

Row 1 (Wrong side)**:** Dc in eighth ch from hook (**7 skipped chs count as first dc plus ch 2 and 2 skipped chs**) and in next 2 chs, ★ ch 4, skip next 4 chs, dc in next 3 chs; repeat from ★ across to last 3 chs, ch 2, skip next 2 chs, dc in last ch.

Note: Loop a short piece of yarn around the **back** of any stitch on Row 1 to mark **right** side.

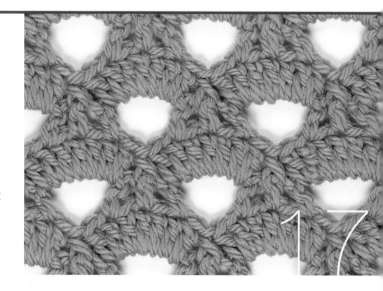

12

To work Front Post single crochet (*abbreviated FPsc*), insert hook from **front** to **back** around post of dc indicated (*Fig. 1, page 79*), YO and pull up a loop, YO and draw through both loops on hook.

Row 2: Ch 3 (**counts as first dc, now and throughout**), turn; 3 dc in next ch-2 sp, skip next dc, work FPsc around next dc, ★ 7 dc in next ch-4 sp, skip next dc, work FPsc around next dc; repeat from ★ across to last ch-2 sp, 3 dc in last ch-2 sp, dc in last dc.

Row 3: Ch 3, turn; skip first 2 dc, dc in next dc, ch 4, skip next 3 sts, dc in next dc, ★ (skip next dc, dc in next dc) twice, ch 4, skip next 3 sts, dc in next dc; repeat from ★ across to last 2 dc, skip next dc, dc in last dc.

Row 4: Ch 1, turn; sc in first dc, 7 dc in next ch-4 sp, ★ skip next dc, work FPsc around next dc, 7 dc in next ch-4 sp; repeat from ★ across to last 2 dc, skip next dc, sc in last dc.

Row 5: Ch 5 (**counts as first dc plus ch 2**), turn; skip first 2 sts, dc in next dc, (skip next dc, dc in next dc) twice, ★ ch 4, skip next 3 sts, dc in next dc, (skip next dc, dc in next dc) twice; repeat from ★ across to last 2 sts, ch 2, skip next dc, dc in last sc.

Repeat Rows 2-5 for pattern.

Flutter

Chain a multiple of 8 + 2 chs.

Row 1 (Right side)**:** Sc in second ch from hook, ★ skip next 3 chs, (2 dc, ch 1, dc, ch 1, 2 dc) in next ch, skip next 3 chs, sc in next ch; repeat from ★ across.

Note: Loop a short piece of yarn around any stitch to mark Row 1 as **right** side.

To work Back Post double crochet (*abbreviated BPdc*), YO, insert hook from **back** to **front** around post of st indicated (*Fig. 1, page 79*), YO and pull up a loop (3 loops on hook), (YO and draw through 2 loops on hook) twice.

Row 2: Ch 3 (**counts as first dc, now and throughout**), turn; 2 dc in next ch-1 sp, ch 1, work BPdc around next dc, ch 1, 2 dc in next ch-1 sp, ★ skip next 2 dc, work BPdc around next sc, 2 dc in next ch-1 sp, ch 1, work BPdc around next dc, ch 1, 2 dc in next ch-1 sp; repeat from ★ across to last 3 sts, skip next 2 dc, dc in last sc.

To work Front Post double crochet (*abbreviated FPdc*), YO, insert hook from **front** to **back** around post of BPdc indicated (*Fig. 1, page 79*), YO and pull up a loop (3 loops on hook), (YO and draw through 2 loops on hook) twice.

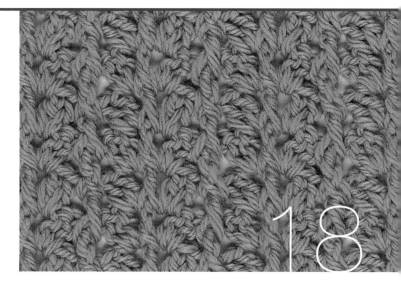

Row 3: Ch 3, turn; 2 dc in next ch-1 sp, ch 1, work FPdc around next BPdc, ch 1, 2 dc in next ch-1 sp, ★ skip next 2 dc, work FPdc around next BPdc, 2 dc in next ch-1 sp, ch 1, work FPdc around next BPdc, ch 1, 2 dc in next ch-1 sp; repeat from ★ across to last 3 dc, skip next 2 dc, dc in last dc.

Row 4: Ch 3, turn; 2 dc in next ch-1 sp, ch 1, work BPdc around next FPdc, ch 1, 2 dc in next ch-1 sp, ★ skip next 2 dc, work BPdc around next FPdc, 2 dc in next ch-1 sp, ch 1, work BPdc around next FPdc, ch 1, 2 dc in next ch-1 sp; repeat from ★ across to last 3 dc, skip next 2 dc, dc in last dc.

Repeat Rows 3 and 4 for pattern.

Alternating Posts

Twists

Chain a multiple of 4 + 5 chs.

Row 1 (Wrong side)**:** Dc in fourth ch from hook (**3 skipped chs count as first dc**) and in each ch across.

Note: Loop a short piece of yarn around the **back** of any stitch on Row 1 to mark **right** side.

To work Front Post double crochet (abbreviated FPdc), YO, insert hook from **front** to **back** around post of dc indicated *(Fig. 1, page 79)*, YO and pull up a loop (3 loops on hook), (YO and draw through 2 loops on hook) twice.

Row 2: Ch 3 (**counts as first dc, now and throughout**), turn; dc in next 2 dc, ★ work FPdc around next dc, dc in next 3 dc; repeat from ★ across.

Row 3: Ch 3, turn; dc in next st and in each st across.

Row 4: Ch 3, turn; work FPdc around next dc, ★ dc in next 3 dc, work FPdc around next dc; repeat from ★ across to last dc, dc in last dc.

Row 5: Ch 3, turn; dc in next st and in each st across.

Repeat Rows 2-5 for pattern.

Chain a multiple of 9 + 3 chs.

Row 1 (Wrong side)**:** Dc in fourth ch from hook (**3 skipped chs count as first dc**) and in next ch, ch 1, skip next ch, dc in next 2 chs, ch 1, ★ skip next ch, dc in next 5 chs, ch 1, skip next ch, dc in next 2 chs, ch 1; repeat from ★ across to last 4 chs, skip next ch, dc in last 3 chs.

Note: Loop a short piece of yarn around the **back** of any stitch on Row 1 to mark **right** side.

To work Front Post double crochet (abbreviated FPdc), YO, insert hook from **front** to **back** around post of dc indicated *(Fig. 1, page 79)*, YO and pull up a loop (3 loops on hook), (YO and draw through 2 loops on hook) twice.

Row 2: Ch 3 (**counts as first dc, now and throughout**), turn; dc in next 2 dc, ch 1, skip next ch and next dc, work FPdc around next dc, working in **front** of FPdc just made, work FPdc around skipped dc, ch 1, ★ dc in next 5 dc, ch 1, skip next ch and next dc, work FPdc around next dc, working in **front** of FPdc just made, work FPdc around skipped dc, ch 1; repeat from ★ across to last 3 dc, dc in last 3 dc.

Row 3: Ch 3, turn; dc in next 2 dc, ch 1, dc in next 2 FPdc, ch 1, ★ dc in next 5 dc, ch 1, dc in next 2 FPdc, ch 1; repeat from ★ across to last 3 dc, dc in last 3 dc.

Repeat Rows 2 and 3 for pattern.

Link Stitch

Chain a multiple of 5 + 7 chs.

Row 1 (Right side)**:** Sc in second ch from hook and in each ch across.

Note: Loop a short piece of yarn around any stitch to mark Row 1 as **right** side.

Row 2: Ch 1, turn; sc in each sc across.

To work Front Post double crochet (abbreviated FPdc), YO, working in **front** of previous row *(Fig. 2, page 80)*, insert hook from **front** to **back** around post of sc indicated *(Fig. 1, page 79)*, YO and pull up a loop (3 loops on hook), (YO and draw through 2 loops on hook) twice. Skip sc behind FPdc.

Row 3: Ch 1, turn; sc in first 5 sc, work FPdc around sc one row **below** next sc, ★ sc in next 4 sc, work FPdc around sc one row **below** next sc; repeat from ★ across to last 5 sc, sc in last 5 sc.

Row 4: Ch 1, turn; sc in each st across.

Row 5: Ch 1, turn; sc in first 4 sc, work FPdc around sc one row **below** next sc, sc in next sc, work FPdc around sc one row **below** next sc, ★ sc in next 2 sc, work FPdc around sc one row **below** next sc, sc in next sc, work FPdc around sc one row **below** next sc; repeat from ★ across to last 4 sc, sc in last 4 sc.

Row 6: Ch 1, turn; sc in each st across.

Repeat Rows 3-6 for pattern.

Arrowhead

Chain a multiple of 4 + 3 chs.

Row 1 (Right side)**:** Dc in fourth ch from hook **(3 skipped chs count as first dc)** and in each ch across.

Note: Loop a short piece of yarn around any stitch to mark Row 1 as **right** side.

Row 2: Ch 1, turn; sc in each dc across.

To work Split Front Post double crochet (abbreviated Split FPdc) (uses 3 dc), YO, working in **front** of previous row *(Fig. 2, page 80)*, insert hook from **front** to **back** around post of dc one row **below** next sc *(Fig. 1, page 79)*, YO and pull up a loop, YO and draw through 2 loops on hook, YO, skip next dc, insert hook from **front** to **back** around post of next dc, YO and pull up a loop, YO and draw through 2 loops on hook, YO and draw through all 3 loops on hook.

Row 3: Ch 4 **(counts as first dc plus ch 1)**, turn; work Split FPdc, ch 1, skip next 3 sc from first dc made, dc in next sc, ★ ch 1, work Split FPdc, ch 1, skip next 3 sc from last dc made, dc in next sc; repeat from ★ across.

Row 4: Ch 1, turn; sc in each st and in each ch-1 sp across.

Row 5: Ch 3 **(counts as first dc)**, turn; dc in next sc and in each sc across.

Row 6: Ch 1, turn; sc in each dc across.

Repeat Rows 3-6 for pattern.

Snuggled Shells

Chain a multiple of 7 + 4 chs.

Row 1 (Right side)**:** Dc in fourth ch from hook **(3 skipped chs count as first dc)**, ★ skip next 2 chs, (3 dc, ch 1, 3 dc) in next ch, skip next 2 chs, dc in next 2 chs; repeat from ★ across.

Note: Loop a short piece of yarn around any stitch to mark Row 1 as **right** side.

To work Back Post double crochet (abbreviated BPdc), YO, insert hook from **back** to **front** around post of st indicated *(Fig. 1, page 79)*, YO and pull up a loop (3 loops on hook), (YO and draw through 2 loops on hook) twice.

Row 2: Ch 4 **(counts as first dc plus ch 1, now and throughout)**, turn; dc in first dc, ch 1, work BPdc around next dc, ch 1, sc in next ch-1 sp, ch 1, skip next 3 dc, work BPdc around next dc, ch 1, ★ (dc, ch 1) twice in sp **before** next dc *(Fig. 3, page 80)*, work BPdc around next dc, ch 1, sc in next ch-1 sp, ch 1, skip next 3 dc, work BPdc around next dc, ch 1; repeat from ★ across to last dc, (dc, ch 1, dc) in last dc.

To work Front Post double crochet (abbreviated FPdc), YO, insert hook from **front** to **back** around post of BPdc indicated *(Fig. 1, page 79)*, YO and pull up a loop (3 loops on hook), (YO and draw through 2 loops on hook) twice.

Row 3: Ch 4, turn; 2 dc in next ch-1 sp, skip next dc, work FPdc around next BPdc, skip next sc, work FPdc around next BPdc, skip next ch-1 sp, ★ (2 dc, ch 3, 2 dc) in next ch-1 sp, skip next dc, work FPdc around next BPdc, skip next sc, work FPdc around next BPdc, skip next ch-1 sp; repeat from ★ across to last ch-1 sp, 2 dc in last ch-1 sp, ch 1, dc in last dc.

Row 4: Ch 4, turn; 3 dc in next ch-1 sp, skip next 2 dc, work BPdc around each of next 2 FPdc, ★ (3 dc, ch 1, 3 dc) in next ch-3 sp, skip next 2 dc, work BPdc around each of next 2 FPdc; repeat from ★ across to last ch-1 sp, 3 dc in last ch-1 sp, ch 1, dc in last dc.

Row 5: Ch 1, turn; sc in first dc, skip next 3 dc, work FPdc around next BPdc, ch 1, (dc, ch 1) twice in sp **before** next BPdc, work FPdc around next BPdc, ★ sc in next ch-1 sp, skip next 3 dc, work FPdc around next BPdc, ch 1, (dc, ch 1) twice in sp **before** next BPdc, work FPdc around next BPdc; repeat from ★ across to last ch-1 sp, skip last ch-1 sp, sc in last dc.

Row 6: Ch 3 **(counts as first dc, now and throughout)**, turn; work BPdc around next FPdc, skip next ch-1 sp, (2 dc, ch 3, 2 dc) in next ch-1 sp, skip next dc, work BPdc around next FPdc, ★ skip next sc, work BPdc around next FPdc, skip next ch-1 sp, (2 dc, ch 3, 2 dc) in next ch-1 sp, skip next dc, work BPdc around next FPdc; repeat from ★ across to last sc, dc in last sc.

Row 7: Ch 3, turn; work FPdc around next BPdc, (3 dc, ch 1, 3 dc) in next ch-3 sp, ★ skip next 2 dc, work FPdc around each of next 2 BPdc, (3 dc, ch 1, 3 dc) in next ch-3 sp; repeat from ★ across to last 4 sts, skip next 2 dc, work FPdc around next BPdc, dc in last dc.

Row 8: Ch 4, turn; dc in first dc, ch 1, work BPdc around next FPdc, ch 1, sc in next ch-1 sp, ch 1, skip next 3 dc, work BPdc around next FPdc, ch 1, ★ (dc, ch 1) twice in sp **before** next FPdc, work BPdc around next FPdc, ch 1, sc in next ch-1 sp, ch 1, skip next 3 dc, work BPdc around next FPdc, ch 1; repeat from ★ across to last dc, (dc, ch 1, dc) in last dc.

Repeat Rows 3-8 for pattern.

Bare Branches

Chain a multiple of 12 + 14 chs.

Row 1 (Right side): Sc in second ch from hook and in each ch across.

Note: Loop a short piece of yarn around any stitch to mark Row 1 as **right** side.

Row 2: Ch 1, turn; sc in each sc across.

To work Front Post double crochet (*abbreviated FPdc*), YO, working in **front** of previous row *(Fig. 2, page 80)*, insert hook from **front** to **back** around post of st indicated *(Fig. 1, page 79)*, YO and pull up a loop (3 loops on hook), (YO and draw through 2 loops on hook) twice. Skip sc behind FPdc.

Row 3: Ch 1, turn; sc in first 6 sc, work FPdc around sc one row **below** next sc, ★ sc in next 5 sc, work FPdc around sc one row **below** next sc; repeat from ★ across to last 6 sc, sc in last 6 sc.

Row 4: Ch 1, turn; sc in each st across.

Row 5: Ch 1, turn; sc in first 4 sc, skip next sc, work FPdc around sc one row **below** next sc, sc in next sc, work FPdc around FPdc one row **below** next sc, sc in next sc, work FPdc around sc 2 rows **below** last sc made, ★ sc in next 3 sc, work FPdc around FPdc one row **below** next sc, sc in next 3 sc, skip next sc, work FPdc around sc one row **below** next sc, sc in next sc, work FPdc around FPdc one row **below** next sc, sc in next sc, work FPdc around sc 2 rows **below** last sc made; repeat from ★ across to last 4 sc, sc in last 4 sc.

Row 6: Ch 1, turn; sc in each st across.

Row 7: Ch 1, turn; sc in first 3 sc, skip next sc, [work FPdc around FPdc one row **below** next sc, sc in next 2 sc] twice, work FPdc around FPdc 2 rows **below** last sc made, ★ sc in next 2 sc, work FPdc around FPdc one row **below** next sc, sc in next 2 sc, skip next sc, [work FPdc around FPdc one row **below** next sc, sc in next 2 sc] twice, work FPdc around FPdc 2 rows **below** last sc made; repeat from ★ across to last 3 sc, sc in last 3 sc.

Row 8: Ch 1, turn; sc in each st across.

Row 9: Ch 1, turn; sc in first 2 sc, skip next sc, [work FPdc around FPdc one row **below** next sc, sc in next 3 sc] twice, work FPdc around FPdc 2 rows **below** last sc made, ★ sc in next sc, work FPdc around FPdc one row **below** next sc, sc in next sc, skip next sc, [work FPdc around FPdc one row **below** next sc, sc in next 3 sc] twice, work FPdc around FPdc 2 rows **below** last sc made; repeat from ★ across to last 2 sc, sc in last 2 sc.

Row 10: Ch 1, turn; sc in each st across.

Row 11: Ch 1, turn; sc in first sc, skip next sc, [work FPdc around FPdc one row **below** next sc, sc in next 4 sc] twice, work FPdc around FPdc 2 rows **below** last sc made, ★ work FPdc around FPdc one row **below** next sc, skip next sc, [work FPdc around FPdc one row **below** next sc, sc in next 4 sc] twice, work FPdc around FPdc 2 rows **below** last sc made; repeat from ★ across to last sc, sc in last sc.

Repeat Rows 4-11 for pattern.

Prong Stitch

Chain a multiple of 8 + 9 chs.

Row 1 (Right side)**:** Dc in fourth ch from hook (**3 skipped chs count as first dc**) and in each ch across.

Note: Loop a short piece of yarn around any stitch to mark Row 1 as **right** side.

Row 2: Ch 1, turn; sc in each dc across.

To work Split Front Post treble crochet (abbreviated Split FPtr), YO twice, working in **front** of previous row (*Fig. 2, page 80*), insert hook from **front** to **back** around post of dc indicated (*Fig. 1, page 79*), YO and pull up a loop, (YO and draw through 2 loops on hook) twice, YO twice, skip next 3 sts, insert hook from **front** to **back** around post of next dc, YO and pull up a loop, (YO and draw through 2 loops on hook) twice, YO and draw through all 3 loops on hook. Skip sc behind Split FPtr.

Row 3: Ch 3 (**counts as first dc, now and throughout**), turn; dc in next 2 sc, work Split FPtr beginning around second dc 2 rows **below,** ★ dc in next 7 sc, skip next 3 dc 2 rows **below,** work Split FPtr beginning around next dc; repeat from ★ across to last 3 sc, dc in last 3 sc.

Row 4: Ch 1, turn; sc in each st across.

Row 5: Ch 3, turn; dc in next 6 sc, work Split FPtr beginning around sixth dc 2 rows **below,** dc in next 7 sc, ★ skip next 3 dc 2 rows **below,** work Split FPtr beginning around next dc, dc in next 7 sc; repeat from ★ across.

Row 6: Ch 1, turn; sc in each st across.

Repeat Rows 3-6 for pattern.

Shell Medley

Chain a multiple of 13 + 1 ch.

Row 1 (Wrong side)**:** Sc in second ch from hook, ch 1, skip next ch, sc in next ch, ch 1, skip next 3 chs, (dc, ch 1) 3 times in next ch, skip next 3 chs, sc in next ch, ★ ch 4, skip next 4 chs, sc in next ch, ch 1, skip next 3 chs, (dc, ch 1) 3 times in next ch, skip next 3 chs, sc in next ch; repeat from ★ across to last 2 chs, ch 1, skip next ch, sc in last ch.

Note: Loop a short piece of yarn around the **back** of any stitch on Row 1 to mark **right** side.

To work Front Post double crochet (abbreviated FPdc), YO, insert hook from **front** to **back** around post of dc indicated (*Fig. 1, page 79*), YO and pull up a loop (3 loops on hook), (YO and draw through 2 loops on hook) twice.

Row 2: Ch 3 (**counts as first dc**), turn; 3 dc in next ch-1 sp, skip next sc and next ch, work FPdc around next dc, ch 3, skip next 2 ch-1 sps, work FPdc around next dc, ★ skip next ch-1 sp, 9 dc in next ch-4 sp, skip next sc and next ch, work FPdc around next dc, ch 3, skip next 2 ch-1 sps, work FPdc around next dc; repeat from ★ across to last 2 ch-1 sps, skip next ch-1 sp, 3 dc in last ch-1 sp, dc in last sc.

Row 3: Ch 1, turn; sc in first dc, ch 1, skip next dc, sc in next dc, ch 1, (dc, ch 1) 3 times in next ch-3 sp, skip next 2 sts, sc in next dc, ★ ch 4, skip next 5 dc, sc in next dc, ch 1, (dc, ch 1) 3 times in next ch-3 sp, skip next 2 sts, sc in next dc; repeat from ★ across to last 2 dc, ch 1, skip next dc, sc in last dc.

Repeat Rows 2 and 3 for pattern.

Suspended X

Note: Uses MC and CC in the following sequence: ★ 2 Rows **each** MC, CC; repeat from ★ for stripe sequence.

With MC, chain a multiple of 8 + 10 chs.

Row 1 (Right side)**:** Sc in second ch from hook and in each ch across.

Note: Loop a short piece of yarn around any stitch to mark Row 1 as **right** side.

Row 2: Ch 3 (**counts as first dc, now and throughout**), turn; dc in next sc and in each sc across; finish off.

To work Front Post treble crochet (abbreviated FPtr), YO twice, working in **front** of previous row *(Fig. 2, page 80)*, insert hook from **front** to **back** around post of sc indicated *(Fig. 1, page 79)*, YO and pull up a loop (4 loops on hook), (YO and draw through 2 loops on hook) 3 times.

Row 3: With **right** side facing, join CC with sc in first dc *(see Joining With Sc, page 79)*; sc in next 2 dc, skip next 2 dc, work FPtr around sc one row **below** next dc, ch 1, work FPtr around sc one row **below** first skipped dc, ★ skip next 3 dc from last sc made, sc in next 5 dc, skip next 2 dc, work FPtr around sc one row **below** next dc, ch 1, work FPtr around sc one row **below** first skipped dc; repeat from ★ across to last 6 dc, skip next 3 dc from last sc made, sc in last 3 dc.

Row 4: Ch 3, turn; dc in next st and in each st and each ch-1 sp across; finish off.

Row 5: With **right** side facing, join MC with sc in first dc; sc in next 6 dc, skip next 2 dc, work FPtr around sc one row **below** next dc, ch 1, work FPtr around sc one row **below** first skipped dc, ★ skip next 3 dc from last sc made, sc in next 5 dc, skip next 2 dc, work FPtr around sc one row **below** next dc, ch 1, work FPtr around sc one row **below** first skipped dc; repeat from ★ across to last 10 dc, skip next 3 dc from last sc made, sc in last 7 dc.

Row 6: Ch 3, turn; dc in next st and in each st and each ch-1 sp across; finish off.

Repeat Rows 3-6 for pattern.

Stand-Out Cable

Chain a multiple of 4 chs.

Row 1 (Wrong side)**:** Hdc in third ch from hook (**2 skipped chs count as first hdc**) and in each ch across.

Note: Loop a short piece of yarn around the **back** of any stitch on Row 1 to mark **right** side.

To work Front Post double crochet Cluster (abbreviated FPdc Cluster), ★ YO, insert hook from **front** to **back** around post of st indicated *(Fig. 1, page 79)*, YO and pull up a loop, YO and draw through 2 loops on hook; repeat from ★ 2 times **more**, YO and draw through all 4 loops on hook. Skip hdc behind FPdc Cluster unless otherwise specified.

Row 2: Ch 2 (**counts as first hdc, now and throughout**), turn; hdc in next 2 hdc, ★ skip next hdc, work FPdc Cluster around next hdc, hdc in hdc just worked around and in next 2 hdc; repeat from ★ across.

Row 3: Ch 2, turn; hdc in next st and in each st across.

Row 4: Ch 2, turn; hdc in next 2 hdc, ★ skip next hdc, working in **front** of previous row *(Fig. 2, page 80)*, work FPdc Cluster around hdc one row **below** next hdc, hdc in next 3 hdc; repeat from ★ across.

Repeat Rows 3 and 4 for pattern.

Third Dimension

Chain a multiple of 4 + 2 chs.

Row 1 (Right side)**:** Sc in second ch from hook, ★ ch 3, skip next 3 chs, sc in next ch; repeat from ★ across.

Note: Loop a short piece of yarn around any stitch to mark Row 1 as **right** side.

Row 2: Ch 3 (**counts as first dc, now and throughout**), turn; dc in first sc, skip next ch-3 sp, (3 dc in next sc, skip next ch-3 sp) across to last sc, 2 dc in last sc.

To work Front Post single crochet (abbreviated FPsc), insert hook from **front** to **back** around post of dc indicated *(Fig. 1, page 79)*, YO and pull up a loop, YO and draw through both loops on hook.

Row 3: Ch 1, turn; sc in first dc, ch 3, ★ skip next 2 dc, work FPsc around next dc, ch 3; repeat from ★ across to last 3 dc, skip next 2 dc, sc in last dc.

Row 4: Ch 3, turn; dc in first sc, skip next ch-3 sp, (3 dc in next FPsc, skip next ch-3 sp) across to last sc, 2 dc in last sc.

Repeat Rows 3 and 4 for pattern.

Crimp Stitch

Chain a multiple of 4 + 3 chs.

Row 1 (Right side)**:** Dc in fourth ch from hook **(3 skipped chs count as first dc)** and in each ch across.

Note: Loop a short piece of yarn around any stitch to mark Row 1 as **right** side.

To work Front Post double crochet *(abbreviated FPdc),* YO, insert hook from **front** to **back** around post of st indicated *(Fig. 1, page 79)*, YO and pull up a loop (3 loops on hook), (YO and draw through 2 loops on hook) twice.

Row 2: Ch 3 **(counts as first dc, now and throughout)**, turn; work FPdc around next dc and around each dc across to last dc, dc in last dc.

Row 3: Ch 3, turn; ★ skip next st, dc in next 2 sts, working in **front** of dc just made, work FPdc around skipped st, dc in next st; repeat from ★ across.

Row 4: Ch 3, turn; work FPdc around next st and around each st across to last dc, dc in last dc.

Repeat Rows 3 and 4 for pattern.

Wrap It Up

Chain a multiple of 4 + 5 chs.

Row 1 (Right side)**:** Dc in fourth ch from hook **(3 skipped chs count as first dc)** and in each ch across.

Note: Loop a short piece of yarn around any stitch to mark Row 1 as **right** side.

To work Front Post Puff Stitch *(abbreviated FP Puff St),* ★ YO, insert hook from **front** to **back** around post of dc indicated *(Fig. 1, page 79)*, YO and pull up a loop; repeat from ★ 2 times **more**, YO and draw through all 7 loops on hook.

Row 2: Ch 3 **(counts as first dc, now and throughout)**, turn; dc in next dc, work FP Puff St around last dc made, ★ (ch 1, skip next dc, dc in next dc) twice, work FP Puff St around last dc made; repeat from ★ across to last dc, dc in last dc.

Row 3: Ch 3, turn; skip next FP Puff St, dc in next dc (same dc FP Puff St is worked around), ★ dc in next ch-1 sp, dc in next dc and in next ch-1 sp, skip next FP Puff St, dc in next dc (same dc FP Puff St is worked around); repeat from ★ across to last dc, dc in last dc.

Repeat Rows 2 and 3 for pattern.

Succession

Chain a multiple of 11 + 3 chs.

Row 1 (Wrong side)**:** Dc in sixth ch from hook (**5 skipped chs count as first dc plus ch 1 and 1 skipped ch**) and in next 6 chs, ch 1, ★ skip next ch, dc in next 2 chs, ch 1, skip next ch, dc in next 7 chs, ch 1; repeat from ★ across to last 2 chs, skip next ch, dc in last ch.

Note: Loop a short piece of yarn around the **back** of any stitch on Row 1 to mark **right** side.

To work Front Post double crochet (*abbreviated FPdc*), YO, insert hook from **front** to **back** around post of st indicated *(Fig. 1, page 79)*, YO and pull up a loop (3 loops on hook), (YO and draw through 2 loops on hook) twice.

Row 2: Ch 3 (**counts as first dc, now and throughout**), turn; 3 dc in first dc, ch 1, skip next ch and next 3 dc, work FPdc around next dc, ch 1, ★ skip next 3 dc and next ch, 4 dc in each of next 2 dc, ch 1, skip next ch and next 3 dc, work FPdc around next dc, ch 1; repeat from ★ across to last 4 dc, skip next 3 dc and next ch, 4 dc in last dc.

To work Back Post double crochet (*abbreviated BPdc*), YO, insert hook from **back** to **front** around post of FPdc indicated *(Fig. 1, page 79)*, YO and pull up a loop (3 loops on hook), (YO and draw through 2 loops on hook) twice.

Row 3: Ch 3, turn; 2 dc in first dc, ch 1, dc in next ch-1 sp, work BPdc around next FPdc, dc in next ch-1 sp, ch 1, ★ skip next 3 dc, 3 dc in each of next 2 dc, ch 1, dc in next ch-1 sp, work BPdc around next FPdc, dc in next ch-1 sp, ch 1; repeat from ★ across to last 4 dc, skip next 3 dc, 3 dc in last dc.

Row 4: Ch 3, turn; dc in first dc, ch 1, dc in next ch-1 sp and in next dc, work FPdc around next BPdc, dc in next dc and in next ch-1 sp, ch 1, ★ skip next 2 dc, 2 dc in each of next 2 dc, ch 1, dc in next ch-1 sp and in next dc, work FPdc around next BPdc, dc in next dc and in next ch-1 sp, ch 1; repeat from ★ across to last 3 dc, skip next 2 dc, 2 dc in last dc.

Row 5: Ch 4 (**counts as first dc plus ch 1**), turn; dc in next ch-1 sp and in next 2 dc, work BPdc around next FPdc, dc in next 2 dc and in next ch-1 sp, ch 1, ★ skip next dc, dc in next 2 dc, ch 1, dc in next ch-1 sp and in next 2 dc, work BPdc around next FPdc, dc in next 2 dc and in next ch-1 sp, ch 1; repeat from ★ across to last 2 dc, skip next dc, dc in last dc.

Row 6: Ch 3, turn; 3 dc in first dc, ch 1, skip next 3 dc, work FPdc around next BPdc, ch 1, ★ skip next 3 dc and next ch, 4 dc in each of next 2 dc, ch 1, skip next 3 dc, work FPdc around next BPdc, ch 1; repeat from ★ across to last 4 dc, skip next 3 dc and next ch, 4 dc in last dc.

Repeat Rows 3-6 for pattern.

Expanding Shells

Chain a multiple of 11 + 10 chs.

Row 1 (Wrong side)**:** Dc in fourth ch from hook
(**3 skipped chs count as first dc**) and in next 6 chs,
★ skip next ch, (dc, ch 1, dc) in next ch, skip next ch,
dc in next 8 chs; repeat from ★ across.

Note: Loop a short piece of yarn around the **back** of any
stitch on Row 1 to mark **right** side.

To work Front Post double crochet (abbreviated FPdc),
YO, insert hook from **front** to **back** around post of
st indicated *(Fig. 1, page 79)*, YO and pull up a loop
(3 loops on hook), (YO and draw through 2 loops on
hook) twice.

Row 2: Ch 3 (**counts as first dc, now and throughout**),
turn; dc in next 6 dc, skip next dc, work FPdc around
next dc, (dc, ch 1, dc) in next ch-1 sp, work FPdc around
next dc, ★ skip next dc, dc in next 6 dc, skip next dc,
work FPdc around next dc, (dc, ch 1, dc) in next ch-1 sp,
work FPdc around next dc; repeat from ★ across to last
8 dc, skip next dc, dc in last 7 dc.

To work Back Post double crochet (abbreviated BPdc),
YO, insert hook from **back** to **front** around post of
FPdc indicated *(Fig. 1, page 79)*, YO and pull up a loop
(3 loops on hook), (YO and draw through 2 loops on
hook) twice.

Row 3: Ch 3, turn; dc in next 5 dc, skip next dc, work
BPdc around next FPdc, (2 dc, ch 1, 2 dc) in next
ch-1 sp, skip next dc, work BPdc around next FPdc,
★ skip next dc, dc in next 4 dc, skip next dc, work BPdc
around next FPdc, (2 dc, ch 1, 2 dc) in next ch-1 sp,
skip next dc, work BPdc around next FPdc; repeat from
★ across to last 7 dc, skip next dc, dc in last 6 dc.

Row 4: Ch 3, turn; dc in next 4 dc, skip next dc, work
FPdc around next BPdc, (3 dc, ch 1, 3 dc) in next
ch-1 sp, skip next 2 dc, work FPdc around next BPdc,
★ skip next dc, dc in next 2 dc, skip next dc, work FPdc
around next BPdc, (3 dc, ch 1, 3 dc) in next ch-1 sp, skip
next 2 dc, work FPdc around next BPdc; repeat from
★ across to last 6 dc, skip next dc, dc in last 5 dc.

Row 5: Ch 3, turn; dc in next 7 sts, ★ (dc, ch 1, dc) in
next ch-1 sp, skip next dc, dc in next 8 sts; repeat from
★ across.

Row 6: Ch 3, turn; dc in next 6 dc, skip next dc, work
FPdc around next dc, (dc, ch 1, dc) in next ch-1 sp, work
FPdc around next dc, ★ skip next dc, dc in next 6 dc,
skip next dc, work FPdc around next dc, (dc, ch 1, dc)
in next ch-1 sp, work FPdc around next dc; repeat from
★ across to last 8 dc, skip next dc, dc in last 7 dc.

Repeat Rows 3-6 for pattern.

Arched Pillars

Chain a multiple of 7 + 3 chs.

Row 1 (Wrong side)**:** Dc in fourth ch from hook
(**3 skipped chs count as first dc**) and in next ch, ch 2,
★ skip next 2 chs, dc in next 5 chs, ch 2; repeat from
★ across to last 5 chs, skip next 2 chs, dc in last 3 chs.

Note: Loop a short piece of yarn around the **back** of any
stitch on Row 1 to mark **right** side.

To work Front Post double crochet (abbreviated FPdc),
YO, insert hook from **front** to **back** around post of
st indicated (***Fig. 1, page 79***), YO and pull up a loop
(3 loops on hook), (YO and draw through 2 loops on
hook) twice.

Row 2: Ch 3 (**counts as first dc, now and throughout**),
turn; 6 dc in next ch-2 sp, ★ skip next 2 dc, work FPdc
around next dc, 6 dc in next ch-2 sp; repeat from
★ across to last 3 dc, skip next 2 dc, dc in last dc.

To work Back Post double crochet (abbreviated BPdc),
YO, insert hook from **back** to **front** around post of
FPdc indicated (***Fig. 1, page 79***), YO and pull up a loop
(3 loops on hook), (YO and draw through 2 loops on
hook) twice.

Row 3: Ch 3, turn; dc in next 2 dc, ch 2, ★ skip next
2 dc, dc in next 2 dc, work BPdc around next FPdc, dc
in next 2 dc, ch 2; repeat from ★ across to last 5 dc, skip
next 2 dc, dc in last 3 dc.

Row 4: Ch 3, turn; 6 dc in next ch-2 sp, ★ skip next
2 dc, work FPdc around next BPdc, 6 dc in next ch-2 sp;
repeat from ★ across to last 3 dc, skip next 2 dc, dc in
last dc.

Repeat Rows 3 and 4 for pattern.

Chinese Puzzle

Chain a multiple of 7 + 4 chs.

To double crochet 5 together (abbreviated dc5tog) (uses
next 5 chs), ★ YO, insert hook in **next** ch, YO and pull
up a loop, YO and draw through 2 loops on hook; repeat
from ★ 4 times **more**, YO and draw through all 6 loops
on hook (**counts as one decrease**).

Row 1 (Right side)**:** 2 Dc in fourth ch from hook
(**3 skipped chs count as first dc**), dc5tog, ch 1, ★ skip
next ch, 5 dc in next ch, dc5tog, ch 1; repeat from
★ across to last 2 chs, skip next ch, 3 dc in last ch.

Note: Loop a short piece of yarn around any stitch to
mark Row 1 as **right** side.

To work Front Post double crochet 2 together (*abbreviated FPdc2tog*) (uses next 2 dc), ★ YO, insert hook from **front** to **back** around post of **next** dc (*Fig. 1, page 79*), YO and pull up a loop, YO and draw through 2 loops on hook; repeat from ★ once **more**, YO and draw through all 3 loops on hook (**counts as one decrease**).

To work Front Post double crochet 5 together (*abbreviated FPdc5tog*) (uses next 5 dc), ★ YO, insert hook from **front** to **back** around post of **next** dc (*Fig. 1, page 79*), YO and pull up a loop, YO and draw through 2 loops on hook; repeat from ★ 4 times **more**, YO and draw through all 6 loops on hook (**counts as one decrease**).

Row 2: Ch 3 (**counts as first dc, now and throughout**), turn; work FPdc2tog, ch 1, 5 dc in next ch, ★ skip next decrease, work FPdc5tog, ch 1, 5 dc in next ch; repeat from ★ across to last 4 sts, skip next decrease, work FPdc2tog, dc in last dc.

Row 3: Ch 3, turn; 2 dc in next decrease, work FPdc5tog, ch 1, ★ 5 dc in next ch, skip next decrease, work FPdc5tog, ch 1; repeat from ★ across to last 2 sts, 2 dc in next decrease, dc in last dc.

Repeat Rows 2 and 3 for pattern.

Left Bank

Chain a multiple of 4 chs.

Row 1 (Right side)**:** Dc in fourth ch from hook (**3 skipped chs count as first dc**) and in each ch across.

Note: Loop a short piece of yarn around any stitch to mark Row 1 as **right** side.

Row 2: Ch 3 (**counts as first dc, now and throughout**), turn; dc in next dc and in each dc across.

To work Front Post double crochet (*abbreviated FPdc*), YO, insert hook from **front** to **back** around post of dc indicated (*Fig. 1, page 79*), YO and pull up a loop (3 loops on hook), (YO and draw through 2 loops on hook) twice.

To work Front Post treble crochet (*abbreviated FPtr*), YO twice, insert hook from **front** to **back** around post of dc indicated (*Fig. 1, page 79*), YO and pull up a loop (4 loops on hook), (YO and draw through 2 loops on hook) 3 times.

To work Front Post double treble crochet (*abbreviated FPdtr*), YO 3 times, insert hook from **front** to **back** around post of dc indicated (*Fig. 1, page 79*), YO and pull up a loop (5 loops on hook), (YO and draw through 2 loops on hook) 4 times.

To work Front Post triple treble crochet (*abbreviated FPtrtr*), YO 4 times, insert hook from **front** to **back** around post of dc indicated (*Fig. 1, page 79*), YO and pull up a loop (6 loops on hook), (YO and draw through 2 loops on hook) 5 times.

Row 3: Ch 3, turn; work (FPdc, FPtr, FPdtr, FPtrtr) around next dc, ★ skip next 3 dc, work (FPdc, FPtr, FPdtr, FPtrtr) around next dc; repeat from ★ across to last 4 dc, skip next 3 dc, dc in last dc.

Rows 4-6: Ch 3, turn; dc in next st and in each st across.

Repeat Rows 3-6 for pattern.

Eccentric

Chain a multiple of 6 + 7 chs.

Row 1 (Wrong side)**:** Dc in fourth ch from hook (**3 skipped chs count as first dc**) and in each ch across.

Note: Loop a short piece of yarn around the **back** of any stitch on Row 1 to mark **right** side.

To work Front Post single crochet (abbreviated FPsc), insert hook from **front** to **back** around post of dc indicated (***Fig. 1, page 79)***, YO and pull up a loop, YO and draw through both loops on hook.

Row 2: Ch 1, turn; sc in first dc, work FPsc around each of next 3 dc, ★ dc in next 3 dc, work FPsc around each of next 3 dc; repeat from ★ across to last dc, sc in last dc.

Row 3: Ch 3 (**counts as first dc, now and throughout**), turn; dc in next st and in each st across.

Row 4: Ch 3, turn; ★ dc in next 3 dc, work FPsc around each of next 3 dc; repeat from ★ across to last 4 dc, dc in last 4 dc.

Row 5: Ch 3, turn; dc in next st and in each st across.

Repeat Rows 2-5 for pattern.

Sculpted Doubles

Chain a multiple of 4 + 5 chs.

Row 1 (Wrong side)**:** (Dc, ch 2, dc) in sixth ch from hook (**5 skipped chs count as first dc and 2 skipped chs**), ★ skip next 3 chs, (dc, ch 2, dc) in next ch; repeat from ★ across to last 3 chs, skip next 2 chs, dc in last ch.

Note: Loop a short piece of yarn around the **back** of any stitch on Row 1 to mark **right** side.

To work Front Post double crochet (abbreviated FPdc), YO, insert hook from **front** to **back** around post of dc indicated (***Fig. 1, page 79)***, YO and pull up a loop (3 loops on hook), (YO and draw through 2 loops on hook) twice.

Row 2: Ch 4 (**counts as first dc plus ch 1**), turn; work FPdc around each of next 2 dc, (ch 2, work FPdc around each of next 2 dc) across to last dc, ch 1, dc in last dc.

Row 3: Ch 3 (**counts as first dc**), turn; skip next ch-1 sp and next FPdc, (dc, ch 2, dc) in sp **before** next FPdc (***Fig. 3, page 80)***, ★ skip next ch-2 sp and next FPdc, (dc, ch 2, dc) in sp **before** next FPdc; repeat from ★ across to last ch-1 sp, skip last ch-1 sp, dc in last dc.

Repeat Rows 2 and 3 for pattern.

Little Waves

Chain a multiple of 8 + 5 chs.

Row 1 (Right side)**:** Dc in fourth ch from hook (**3 skipped chs count as first dc**) and in next dc, ★ skip next 2 chs, (2 dc, ch 1, 2 dc) in next ch, skip next 2 chs, dc in next 3 chs; repeat from ★ across.

Note: Loop a short piece of yarn around any stitch to mark Row 1 as **right** side.

To work Front Post double crochet (abbreviated FPdc), YO, insert hook from **front** to **back** around post of st indicated *(Fig. 1, page 79)*, YO and pull up a loop (3 loops on hook), (YO and draw through 2 loops on hook) twice.

Row 2: Ch 3 (**counts as first dc**), turn; work FPdc around each of next 2 sts, (2 dc, ch 1, 2 dc) in next ch-1 sp, ★ skip next 2 dc, work FPdc around each of next 3 sts, (2 dc, ch 1, 2 dc) in next ch-1 sp; repeat from ★ across to last 5 sts, skip next 2 dc, work FPdc around each of next 2 sts, dc in last dc.

Repeat Row 2 for pattern.

Loose Waves

Chain a multiple of 19 + 3 chs.

Row 1 (Wrong side)**:** 4 Dc in fourth ch from hook (**3 skipped chs count as first dc**), dc in next ch, (skip next ch, dc in next ch) 8 times, ★ 5 dc in each of next 2 chs, dc in next ch, (skip next ch, dc in next ch) 8 times; repeat from ★ across to last ch, 5 dc in last ch.

Note: Loop a short piece of yarn around the **back** of any stitch on Row 1 to mark **right** side.

To work Front Post double crochet (abbreviated FPdc), YO, insert hook from **front** to **back** around post of dc indicated *(Fig. 1, page 79)*, YO and pull up a loop (3 loops on hook), (YO and draw through 2 loops on hook) twice.

Row 2: Ch 2 (**counts as first hdc**), turn; work FPdc around next dc and around each dc across to last dc, hdc in last dc.

Row 3: Ch 3 (**counts as first dc**), turn; 4 dc in first hdc, dc in next FPdc, (skip next FPdc, dc in next FPdc) 8 times, ★ 5 dc in each of next 2 FPdc, dc in next FPdc, (skip next FPdc, dc in next FPdc) 8 times; repeat from ★ across to last hdc, 5 dc in last hdc.

Repeat Rows 2 and 3 for pattern.

Partners

Chain a multiple of 10 + 3 chs.

Row 1 (Wrong side): Dc in fourth ch from hook **(3 skipped chs count as first dc)** and in next ch, skip next 2 chs, 5 dc in next ch, ★ skip next 2 chs, dc in next 5 chs, skip next 2 chs, 5 dc in next ch; repeat from ★ across to last 5 chs, skip next 2 chs, dc in last 3 chs.

Note: Loop a short piece of yarn around the **back** of any stitch on Row 1 to mark **right** side.

To work Front Post double crochet (abbreviated FPdc), YO, insert hook from **front** to **back** around post of st indicated *(Fig. 1, page 79)*, YO and pull up a loop (3 loops on hook), (YO and draw through 2 loops on hook) twice.

To work Back Post double crochet (abbreviated BPdc), YO, insert hook from **back** to **front** around post of st indicated *(Fig. 1, page 79)*, YO and pull up a loop (3 loops on hook), (YO and draw through 2 loops on hook) twice.

To work Front Post double crochet 5 together (abbreviated FPdc5tog) (uses next 5 dc), ★ YO, insert hook from **front** to **back** around post of **next** dc *(Fig. 1, page 79)*, YO and pull up a loop, YO and draw through 2 loops on hook; repeat from ★ 4 times **more**, YO and draw through all 6 loops on hook.

Row 2: Ch 2 **(counts as first hdc, now and throughout)**, turn; work FPdc around next dc, work BPdc around next dc, ch 2, work FPdc5tog, ch 2, work BPdc around next dc, ★ (work FPdc around next dc, work BPdc around next dc) twice, ch 2, work FPdc5tog, ch 2, work BPdc around next dc; repeat from ★ across to last 2 dc, work FPdc around next dc, hdc in last dc.

Row 3: Ch 2, turn; work FPdc around next FPdc, work BPdc around next BPdc, skip next ch, 5 dc in next ch, skip next ch-2 sp, work BPdc around next BPdc, ★ (work FPdc around next FPdc, work BPdc around next BPdc) twice, skip next ch, 5 dc in next ch, skip next ch-2 sp, work BPdc around next BPdc; repeat from ★ across to last 2 sts, work FPdc around next FPdc, hdc in last hdc.

Row 4: Ch 2, turn; work FPdc around next FPdc, work BPdc around next BPdc, ch 2, work FPdc5tog, ch 2, work BPdc around next BPdc, ★ (work FPdc around next FPdc, work BPdc around next BPdc) twice, ch 2, work FPdc5tog, ch 2, work BPdc around next BPdc; repeat from ★ across to last 2 sts, work FPdc around next FPdc, hdc in last hdc.

Repeat Rows 3 and 4 for pattern.

Stand-Out Boxes

Note: Uses Color A, Color B, and Color C in the following sequence: 2 Rows Color A, ★ 2 rows Color B, 4 rows Color C, 2 rows Color B, 2 rows Color A; repeat from ★ for sequence.

With Color A, chain a multiple of 10 + 5 chs.

Row 1 (Right side)**:** Sc in second ch from hook and in each ch across.

Note: Loop a short piece of yarn around any stitch to mark Row 1 as **right** side.

Row 2: Ch 1, turn; sc in each sc across; finish off.

Row 3: With **right** side facing, join Color B with sc in first sc *(see Joining With Sc, page 79)*; sc in next sc and in each sc across.

Row 4: Ch 1, turn; sc in each sc across; finish off.

Row 5: With **right** side facing, join Color C with sc in first sc; sc in next sc and in each sc across.

Rows 6-8: Ch 1, turn; sc in each sc across; at end of Row 8, finish off.

To work Front Post treble crochet (abbreviated FPtr), YO twice, working in **front** of previous rows *(Fig. 2, page 80)*, insert hook from **front** to **back** around post of sc indicated *(Fig. 1, page 79)*, YO and pull up a loop (4 loops on hook), (YO and draw through 2 loops on hook) 3 times. Skip sc behind FPtr.

Row 9: With **right** side facing, join Color B with sc in first sc; ★ sc in next 2 sc, work FPtr around sc 4 rows **below** each of next 2 sc, sc in next 4 sc, work FPtr around sc 4 rows **below** each of next 2 sc; repeat from ★ across to last 3 sc, sc in last 3 sc.

Row 10: Ch 1, turn; sc in each st across; finish off.

To work Front Post triple treble crochet (abbreviated FPtrtr), YO 4 times, working in **front** of previous rows *(Fig. 2, page 80)*, insert hook from **front** to **back** around post of sc indicated *(Fig. 1, page 79)*, YO and pull up a loop (6 loops on hook), (YO and draw through 2 loops on hook) 5 times. Skip sc behind FPtrtr.

Row 11: With **right** side facing, join Color A with sc in first sc; work FPtrtr around sc 8 rows **below** each of next 2 sc, ★ sc in next 8 sc, work FPtrtr around sc 8 rows **below** each of next 2 sc; repeat from ★ across to last sc, sc in last sc.

Repeat Rows 2-11 for pattern.

Crossover

Chain a multiple of 3 + 4 chs.

Row 1 (Wrong side)**:** Sc in second ch from hook and in next ch, ch 2, ★ skip next 2 chs, sc in next ch, ch 2; repeat from ★ across to last 4 chs, skip next 2 chs, sc in last 2 chs.

Note: Loop a short piece of yarn around the **back** of any stitch on Row 1 to mark **right** side.

To work Front Post treble crochet (*abbreviated FPtr*), YO twice, insert hook from **front** to **back** around post of sc indicated (*Fig. 1, page 79*), YO and pull up a loop (4 loops on hook), (YO and draw through 2 loops on hook) 3 times.

Row 2: Ch 4 (**counts as first dc plus ch 1, now and throughout**), turn; ★ skip next sc, 3 dc in next ch-2 sp, working in **front** of dc just made, work FPtr around skipped sc; repeat from ★ across to last 2 sc, skip next sc, dc in last sc.

Row 3: Ch 1, turn; sc in first dc and in sp **before** next FPtr (*Fig. 3, page 80*), ch 2, ★ skip next 4 sts, sc in sp **before** next FPtr, ch 2; repeat from ★ across to last 5 sts, skip next 4 sts, sc in next ch-1 sp and in last dc.

Row 4: Ch 4, turn; skip next sc and next ch-2 sp, work FPtr around next sc, working **behind** FPtr just made, work 3 dc in skipped ch-2 sp, ★ skip next ch-2 sp, work FPtr around next sc, working **behind** FPtr just made, work 3 dc in skipped ch-2 sp; repeat from ★ across to last sc, dc in last sc.

Row 5: Ch 1, turn; sc in first dc and in sp **before** next dc, ch 2, ★ skip next 4 sts, sc in sp **before** next dc, ch 2; repeat from ★ across to last 5 sts, skip next 4 sts, sc in next ch-1 sp and in last dc.

Repeat Rows 2-5 for pattern.

Dip Stitch

Note: Uses MC and CC in the following sequence: ★ 2 Rows **each** MC, CC; repeat from ★ for stripe sequence.

With MC, chain a multiple of 4 chs.

Row 1 (Right side)**:** Sc in second ch from hook and in each ch across.

Note: Loop a short piece of yarn around any stitch to mark Row 1 as **right** side.

Row 2: Ch 2 (**counts as first hdc, now and throughout**), turn; hdc in next sc and in each sc across; finish off.

To work Front Post double crochet (abbreviated FPdc), YO, working in **front** of previous row *(Fig. 2, page 80)*, insert hook from **front** to **back** around post of sc indicated *(Fig. 1, page 79)*, YO and pull up a loop (3 loops on hook), (YO and draw through 2 loops on hook) twice. Skip hdc behind FPdc.

Row 3: With **right** side facing, join CC with sc in first hdc *(see Joining With Sc, page 79)*; sc in next 2 hdc, ★ work FPdc around sc one row **below** next hdc, sc in next 3 hdc; repeat from ★ across.

Row 4: Ch 2, turn; hdc in next st and in each st across; finish off.

Row 5: With **right** side facing, join MC with sc in first hdc; work FPdc around sc one row **below** next hdc, ★ sc in next 3 hdc, work FPdc around sc one row **below** next hdc; repeat from ★ across to last hdc, sc in last hdc.

Row 6: Ch 2, turn; hdc in next st and in each st across; finish off.

Repeat Rows 3-6 for pattern.

X Stitch

Note: Uses MC and CC in the following sequence: ★ 2 Rows **each** MC, CC; repeat from ★ for stripe sequence.

With MC, chain a multiple of 4 + 2 chs.

Row 1 (Right side)**:** Sc in second ch from hook and in each ch across.

Note: Loop a short piece of yarn around any stitch to mark Row 1 as **right** side.

Row 2: Ch 3 (**counts as first dc, now and throughout**), turn; dc in next sc, ch 1, ★ skip next sc, dc in next sc, ch 1; repeat from ★ across to last 3 sc, skip next sc, dc in last 2 sc; finish off.

Row 3: With **right** side facing, join CC with dc in first dc *(see Joining With Dc, page 79)*; dc in next dc and in each ch-1 sp and each dc across.

Row 4: Ch 3, turn; dc in next dc and in each dc across; finish off.

To work Front Post double treble crochet (abbreviated FPdtr) YO 3 times, working in **front** of previous rows *(Fig. 2, page 80)*, insert hook from **front** to **back** around post of dc indicated *(Fig. 1, page 79)*, YO and pull up a loop (5 loops on hook), (YO and draw through 2 loops on hook) 4 times.

Row 5: With **right** side facing, join MC with sc in first dc *(see Joining With Sc, page 79)*; ★ skip next 2 dc, work FPdtr around dc 2 rows **below** next dc, ch 1, working in **front** of last FPdtr made, work FPdtr around dc 2 rows **below** first skipped dc, skip next 3 dc from last sc made, sc in next dc; repeat from ★ across.

Row 6: Ch 3, turn; dc in next FPdtr, ch 1, skip next ch-1 sp, ★ dc in next FPdtr, ch 1, skip next sc, dc in next FPdtr, ch 1, skip next ch-1 sp; repeat from ★ across to last 2 sts, dc in last 2 sts; finish off.

Repeat Rows 3-6 for pattern.

In Depth

Chain a multiple of 3 + 2 chs.

Row 1 (Wrong side)**:** Sc in second ch from hook, ★ ch 2, skip next 2 chs, sc in next ch; repeat from ★ across.

Note: Loop a short piece of yarn around the **back** of any stitch on Row 1 to mark **right** side.

To work Front Post double crochet (abbreviated FPdc), YO, insert hook from **front** to **back** around post of st indicated *(Fig. 1, page 79)*, YO and pull up a loop (3 loops on hook), (YO and draw through 2 loops on hook) twice.

Row 2: Ch 3 (**counts as first dc, now and throughout**), turn; 2 dc in next ch-2 sp, (work FPdc around next sc, 2 dc in next ch-2 sp) across to last sc, dc in last sc.

Row 3: Ch 1, turn; sc in first dc, ★ ch 2, skip next 2 dc, sc in next st; repeat from ★ across.

Row 4: Ch 3, turn; 2 dc in next ch-2 sp, ★ working in **front** of previous row *(Fig. 2, page 80)*, work FPdc around FPdc one row **below** next sc, 2 dc in next ch-2 sp; repeat from ★ across to last sc, dc in last sc.

Repeat Rows 3 and 4 for pattern.

Parallel Lines

Chain a multiple of 5 + 6 chs.

Row 1 (Wrong side)**:** Dc in fourth ch from hook (**3 skipped chs count as first dc**) and in each ch across.

Note: Loop a short piece of yarn around the **back** of any stitch on Row 1 to mark **right** side.

To work Front Post double crochet (abbreviated FPdc), YO, insert hook from **front** to **back** around post of st indicated *(Fig. 1, page 79)*, YO and pull up a loop (3 loops on hook), (YO and draw through 2 loops on hook) twice.

Row 2: Ch 1, turn; sc in first 4 dc, ★ work FPdc around next dc, sc in next 4 dc; repeat from ★ across.

Row 3: Ch 3 (**counts as first dc**), turn; dc in next st and in each st across.

Row 4: Ch 1, turn; sc in first 4 dc, ★ working in **front** of previous row *(Fig. 2, page 80)*, work FPdc around FPdc one row **below** next dc, skip dc behind FPdc, sc in next 4 dc; repeat from ★ across.

Repeat Rows 3 and 4 for pattern.

Up & Down

Chain a multiple of 2 + 5 chs.

Row 1 (Right side)**:** Dc in fourth ch from hook (**3 skipped chs count as first dc**) and in each ch across.

Note: Loop a short piece of yarn around any stitch to mark Row 1 as **right** side.

Row 2: Ch 1, turn; sc in each dc across.

To work Front Post double crochet (abbreviated FPdc), YO, working in **front** of previous row *(Fig. 2, page 80)*, insert hook from **front** to **back** around post of dc indicated *(Fig. 1, page 79)*, YO and pull up a loop (3 loops on hook), (YO and draw through 2 loops on hook) twice. Skip sc behind FPdc.

Row 3: Ch 3 (**counts as first dc, now and throughout**), turn; work FPdc around dc one row **below** next sc, ★ dc in next sc, work FPdc around dc one row **below** next sc; repeat from ★ across to last sc, dc in last sc.

Row 4: Ch 1, turn; sc in each st across.

Row 5: Ch 3, turn; ★ dc in next sc, work FPdc around dc one row **below** next sc; repeat from ★ across to last 2 sc, dc in last 2 sc.

Row 6: Ch 1, turn; sc in each st across.

Repeat Rows 3-6 for pattern.

Slider

Chain a multiple of 3 + 4 chs.

Row 1 (Right side)**:** Dc in sixth ch from hook (**5 skipped chs count as first dc and 2 skipped chs**), ch 1, working **around** dc just made, dc in fourth skipped ch, ★ skip next 2 chs, dc in next ch, ch 1, working **around** dc just made, dc in first skipped ch; repeat from ★ across to last ch, dc in last ch.

Note: Loop a short piece of yarn around any stitch to mark Row 1 as **right** side.

Row 2: Ch 1, turn; sc in each dc and in each ch-1 sp across.

To work Front Post double crochet (abbreviated FPdc), YO, working in **front** of previous row *(Fig. 2, page 80)*, insert hook from **front** to **back** around post of dc indicated *(Fig. 1, page 79)*, YO and pull up a loop (3 loops on hook), (YO and draw through 2 loops on hook) twice.

Row 3: Ch 3 (**counts as first dc**), turn; ★ skip next 2 sc, dc in next sc, ch 1, work FPdc around dc one row **below** first skipped sc; repeat from ★ across to last sc, dc in last sc.

Row 4: Ch 1, turn; sc in each st and in each ch-1 sp across.

Repeat Rows 3 and 4 for pattern.

Corded X's

Chain a multiple of 8 + 2 chs.

Row 1 (Wrong side)**:** Dc in fourth ch from hook
(**3 skipped chs count as first dc**) and in next ch, skip
next ch, dc in next ch, working in **front** of dc just made,
dc in skipped ch, ★ dc in next 6 chs, skip next ch, dc in
next ch, working in **front** of dc just made, dc in skipped
ch; repeat from ★ across to last 3 chs, dc in last 3 chs.

Note: Loop a short piece of yarn around the **back** of any
stitch on Row 1 to mark **right** side.

To work Front Post double crochet (abbreviated FPdc),
YO, insert hook from **front** to **back** around post of
st indicated *(Fig. 1, page 79)*, YO and pull up a loop
(3 loops on hook), (YO and draw through 2 loops on
hook) twice.

Row 2: Ch 3 (**counts as first dc, now and throughout**),
turn; dc in next dc, work FPdc around next dc, skip
next dc, work FPdc around next dc, working in **front**
of FPdc just made, work FPdc around skipped dc, work
FPdc around next dc, ★ dc in next 4 dc, work FPdc
around next dc, skip next dc, work FPdc around next dc,
working in **front** of FPdc just made, work FPdc around
skipped dc, work FPdc around next dc; repeat from
★ across to last 2 dc, dc in last 2 dc.

To work Back Post double crochet (abbreviated BPdc),
YO, insert hook from **back** to **front** around post of
FPdc indicated *(Fig. 1, page 79)*, YO and pull up a loop
(3 loops on hook), (YO and draw through 2 loops on
hook) twice.

Row 3: Ch 3, turn; dc in next dc, work BPdc around
next FPdc, skip next FPdc, work BPdc around next
FPdc, working **behind** FPdc just made, work BPdc
around skipped FPdc, work BPdc around next FPdc,
★ dc in next 4 dc, work BPdc around next FPdc, skip
next FPdc, work BPdc around next FPdc, working
behind FPdc just made, work BPdc around skipped
FPdc, work BPdc around next FPdc; repeat from
★ across to last 2 dc, dc in last 2 dc.

Row 4: Ch 3, turn; dc in next dc, work FPdc around
next BPdc, skip next BPdc, work FPdc around next
BPdc, working in **front** of FPdc just made, work FPdc
around skipped BPdc, work FPdc around next BPdc,
★ dc in next 4 dc, work FPdc around next BPdc, skip
next BPdc, work FPdc around next BPdc, working in
front of FPdc just made, work FPdc around skipped
BPdc, work FPdc around next BPdc; repeat from
★ across to last 2 dc, dc in last 2 dc.

Repeat Rows 3 and 4 for pattern.

Granada

Chain a multiple of 11 + 4 chs.

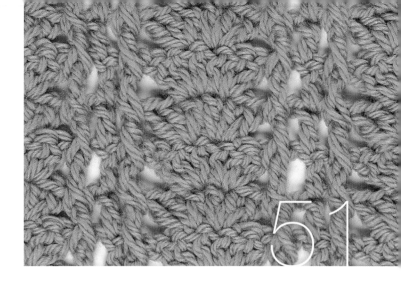

Row 1 (Right side): 3 Dc in fourth ch from hook (**3 skipped chs count as first dc**), skip next 2 chs, dc in next ch, (ch 1, skip next ch, dc in next ch) twice, ★ skip next 2 chs, 3 dc in each of next 2 chs, skip next 2 chs, dc in next ch, (ch 1, skip next ch, dc in next ch) twice; repeat from ★ across to last 4 chs, skip next 2 chs, 3 dc in next ch, dc in last ch.

Note: Loop a short piece of yarn around any stitch to mark Row 1 as **right** side.

To work Back Post double crochet (abbreviated BPdc), YO, insert hook from **back** to **front** around post of st indicated (*Fig. 1, page 79*), YO and pull up a loop (3 loops on hook), (YO and draw through 2 loops on hook) twice.

Row 2: Ch 3 (**counts as first dc, now and throughout**), turn; 3 dc in next dc, skip next 2 dc, work BPdc around next dc, ch 1, dc in next dc, ch 1, work BPdc around next dc, ★ skip next 2 dc, 3 dc in each of next 2 dc, skip next 2 dc, work BPdc around next dc, ch 1, dc in next dc, ch 1, work BPdc around next dc; repeat from ★ across to last 4 dc, skip next 2 dc, 3 dc in next dc, dc in last dc.

To work Front Post double crochet (abbreviated FPdc), YO, insert hook from **front** to **back** around post of BPdc indicated (*Fig. 1, page 79*), YO and pull up a loop (3 loops on hook), (YO and draw through 2 loops on hook) twice.

Row 3: Ch 3, turn; 3 dc in next dc, skip next 2 dc, work FPdc around next BPdc, ch 1, dc in next dc, ch 1, work FPdc around next BPdc, ★ skip next 2 dc, 3 dc in each of next 2 dc, skip next 2 dc, work FPdc around next BPdc, ch 1, dc in next dc, ch 1, work FPdc around next BPdc; repeat from ★ across to last 4 dc, skip next 2 dc, 3 dc in next dc, dc in last dc.

Row 4: Ch 3, turn; 3 dc in next dc, skip next 2 dc, work BPdc around next FPdc, ch 1, dc in next dc, ch 1, work BPdc around next FPdc, ★ skip next 2 dc, 3 dc in each of next 2 dc, skip next 2 dc, work BPdc around next FPdc, ch 1, dc in next dc, ch 1, work BPdc around next FPdc; repeat from ★ across to last 4 dc, skip next 2 dc, 3 dc in next dc, dc in last dc.

Repeat Rows 3 and 4 for pattern.

Spaced X's

Chain a multiple of 8 + 5 chs.

Row 1 (Right side)**:** Sc in second ch from hook and in each ch across.

Note: Loop a short piece of yarn around any stitch to mark Row 1 as **right** side.

Row 2: Ch 3 (**counts as first dc, now and throughout**), turn; dc in next sc and in each sc across.

To work Front Post double crochet (abbreviated FPdc), YO, working in **front** of previous row *(Fig. 2, page 80)*, insert hook from **front** to **back** around post of sc indicated *(Fig. 1, page 79)*, YO and pull up a loop (3 loops on hook), (YO and draw through 2 loops on hook) twice. Skip dc behind FPdc.

Row 3: Ch 1, turn; sc in first dc, skip next dc, work FPdc around sc one row **below** next dc, working in **front** of last FPdc made, work FPdc around sc one row **below** skipped dc, ★ sc in next 6 dc, skip next dc, work FPdc around sc one row **below** next dc, working in **front** of last FPdc made, work FPdc around sc one row **below** skipped dc; repeat from ★ across to last dc, sc in last dc.

Row 4: Ch 3, turn; dc in next st and in each st across.

Row 5: Ch 1, turn; sc in first 5 dc, skip next dc, work FPdc around sc one row **below** next dc, working in **front** of FPdc just made, work FPdc around sc one row **below** skipped dc, ★ sc in next 6 dc, skip next dc, work FPdc around sc one row **below** next dc, working in **front** of FPdc just made, work FPdc around sc one row **below** skipped dc; repeat from ★ across to last 5 dc, sc in last 5 dc.

Row 6: Ch 3, turn; dc in next st and in each st across.

Repeat Rows 3-6 for pattern.

X Columns

Chain a multiple of 5 chs.

To treble crochet (abbreviated tr), YO twice, insert hook in st indicated, YO and pull up a loop (4 loops on hook), (YO and draw through 2 loops on hook) 3 times.

Row 1 (Right side)**:** Tr in fifth ch from hook (**4 skipped chs count as first tr**), ★ skip next 2 chs, tr in next ch, ch 1, working in **front** of last tr made, tr in first skipped ch, tr in next 2 chs; repeat from ★ across.

Note: Loop a short piece of yarn around any stitch to mark Row 1 as **right** side.

Row 2: Ch 1, turn; sc in each tr and in each ch-1 sp across.

To work Front Post treble crochet (abbreviated FPtr), YO twice, working in **front** of previous row *(Fig. 2, page 80)*, insert hook from **front** to **back** around post of st indicated *(Fig. 1, page 79)*, YO and pull up a loop (4 loops on hook), (YO and draw through 2 loops on hook) 3 times. Skip sc behind FPtr.

Row 3: Ch 4 (**counts as first tr**), turn; work FPtr around st one row **below** next sc, ★ † skip next 2 sc, tr in next sc, ch 1, working in **front** of last tr made, tr in first skipped sc †, work FPtr around st one row **below** each of next 2 sc; repeat from ★ across to last 5 sc, then repeat from † to † once, work FPtr around st one row **below** next sc, tr in last sc.

Row 4: Ch 1, turn; sc in each st and in each ch-1 sp across.

Repeat Rows 3 and 4 for pattern.

Horizontal Chevrons

Chain a multiple of 6 + 3 chs.

Row 1 (Wrong side)**:** Sc in second ch from hook and in each ch across.

Note: Loop a short piece of yarn around the **back** of any stitch on Row 1 to mark **right** side.

Row 2: Ch 1, turn; sc in first 2 sc, place marker around sc just made, sc in next sc and in each sc across.

Row 3: Ch 1, turn; sc in each sc across.

To work Front Post treble crochet (abbreviated FPtr), YO twice, working in **front** of previous row *(Fig. 2, page 80)*, insert hook from **front** to **back** around post of st indicated *(Fig. 1, page 79)*, YO and pull up a loop (4 loops on hook), (YO and draw through 2 loops on hook) 3 times. Skip sc behind FPtr.

Row 4: Ch 1, turn; sc in first 6 sc, work FPtr around marked sc 2 rows **below**, remove marker, ★ sc in next 2 sc on previous row, skip next 2 sc 2 rows **below**, work FPtr around next sc; repeat from ★ across to last sc on previous row, sc in last sc.

Row 5: Ch 1, turn; sc in each st across.

Row 6: Ch 1, turn; sc in first sc, work FPtr around next FPtr 2 rows **below**, ★ sc in next 2 sc on previous row, work FPtr around next FPtr 2 rows **below**; repeat from ★ across to last 6 sc on previous row, sc in last 6 sc.

Rows 7-9: Ch 1, turn; sc in each st across.

Row 10: Ch 1, turn; sc in first 2 sc, place marker around sc just made, sc in next sc and in each sc across.

Row 11: Ch 1, turn; sc in each sc across.

Repeat Rows 4-11 for pattern.

Diagonal Dip

Chain a multiple of 2 + 3 chs.

Row 1 (Wrong side)**:** Hdc in third ch from hook (**2 skipped chs count as first hdc**) and in each ch across.

Note: Loop a short piece of yarn around the **back** of any stitch on Row 1 to mark **right** side.

To work Front Post double crochet (abbreviated FPdc), YO, insert hook from **front** to **back** around post of hdc indicated (***Fig. 1, page 79***), YO and pull up a loop (3 loops on hook), (YO and draw through 2 loops on hook) twice.

Row 2: Ch 2 (**counts as first hdc, now and throughout**), turn; ★ skip next hdc, hdc in next hdc, working in **front** of hdc just made, work FPdc around skipped hdc; repeat from ★ across to last hdc, hdc in last hdc.

Row 3: Ch 2, turn; hdc in next st and in each st across.

Repeat Rows 2 and 3 for pattern.

Post Clusters

Chain a multiple of 2 chs.

Row 1 (Wrong side)**:** Hdc in third ch from hook (**2 skipped chs count as first hdc**) and in each ch across.

Note: Loop a short piece of yarn around the **back** of any stitch on Row 1 to mark **right** side.

To work Front Post double crochet Cluster (abbreviated FPdc Cluster) (uses one hdc), ★ YO, insert hook from **front** to **back** around post of hdc indicated (***Fig. 1, page 79***), YO and pull up a loop, YO and draw through 2 loops on hook; repeat from ★ once **more**, YO and draw through all 3 loops on hook.

Row 2: Ch 2 (**counts as first hdc, now and throughout**), turn; work FPdc Cluster around next hdc, ★ ch 1, skip next hdc, work FPdc Cluster around next hdc; repeat from ★ across to last hdc, hdc in last hdc.

Row 3: Ch 2, turn; hdc in each st and in each ch-1 sp across.

Repeat Rows 2 and 3 for pattern.

Simple Rib

Chain a multiple of 2 + 4 chs.

Row 1 (Right side)**:** Dc in fourth ch from hook
(**3 skipped chs count as first dc**) and in each ch across.

Note: Loop a short piece of yarn around any stitch to
mark Row 1 as **right** side.

To work Front Post double crochet (abbreviated FPdc),
YO, insert hook from **front** to **back** around post of
st indicated (***Fig. 1, page 79***), YO and pull up a loop
(3 loops on hook), (YO and draw through 2 loops on
hook) twice.

To work Back Post double crochet (abbreviated BPdc),
YO, insert hook from **back** to **front** around post of
st indicated (***Fig. 1, page 79***), YO and pull up a loop
(3 loops on hook), (YO and draw through 2 loops on
hook) twice.

Row 2: Ch 2 (**counts as first hdc**), turn; (work FPdc
around next st, work BPdc around next st) across to last
st, hdc in last st.

Repeat Row 2 for pattern.

Spaced Wraps

Chain a multiple of 4 + 8 chs.

Row 1 (Wrong side)**:** Dc in sixth ch from hook
(**5 skipped chs count as first dc plus ch 1 and 1 skipped
chs**), ★ ch 1, skip next ch, dc in next ch; repeat from
★ across.

Note: Loop a short piece of yarn around the **back** of any
stitch on Row 1 to mark **right** side.

To work Front Post double crochet (abbreviated FPdc),
YO, insert hook from **front** to **back** around post of
dc indicated (***Fig. 1, page 79***), YO and pull up a loop
(3 loops on hook), (YO and draw through 2 loops on
hook) twice.

Row 2: Ch 1, turn; sc in first dc, (work 3 FPdc around
next dc, sc in next dc) across.

Row 3: Ch 4 (**counts as first dc plus ch 1**), turn; skip
next FPdc, dc in next FPdc, ★ ch 1, skip next FPdc, dc in
next st; repeat from ★ across.

Repeat Rows 2 and 3 for pattern.

Diamond Columns

Chain a multiple of 6 + 3 chs.

Row 1 (Wrong side)**:** Dc in fourth ch from hook (**3 skipped chs count as first dc**) and in each ch across.

Note: Loop a short piece of yarn around the **back** of any stitch on Row 1 to mark **right** side.

To work Front Post double crochet (*abbreviated FPdc*)**,** YO, insert hook from **front** to **back** around post of st indicated (*Fig. 1, page 79*), YO and pull up a loop (3 loops on hook), (YO and draw through 2 loops on hook) twice.

Row 2: Ch 1, turn; sc in first 3 dc, work FPdc around next dc, (sc in next 5 dc, work FPdc around next dc) across to last 3 dc, sc in last 3 dc.

Row 3: Ch 3 (**counts as first dc, now and throughout**), turn; dc in next st and in each st across.

Row 4: Ch 1, turn; sc in first 3 dc, working in **front** of previous row (*Fig. 2, page 80*), work FPdc around FPdc one row **below** next dc, skip dc behind FPdc just made, ★ sc in next 5 dc, working in **front** of previous row, work FPdc around FPdc one row **below** next dc, skip dc behind FPdc just made; repeat from ★ across to last 3 dc, sc in last 3 dc.

Row 5: Ch 3, turn; dc in next st and in each st across.

Row 6: Ch 1, turn; sc in first 2 dc, work FPdc around next dc, working in **front** of previous row, work FPdc around FPdc one row **below** next dc, skip dc behind FPdc just made, work FPdc around next dc, ★ sc in next 3 dc, work FPdc around next dc, working in **front** of previous row, work FPdc around FPdc one row **below** next dc, skip dc behind FPdc just made, work FPdc around next dc; repeat from ★ across to last 2 dc, sc in last 2 dc.

Row 7: Ch 3, turn; dc in next st and in each st across.

Row 8: Ch 1, turn; sc in first dc, ★ work FPdc around next dc, working in **front** of previous row, work FPdc around FPdc one row **below** each of next 3 dc, skip each dc behind FPdc just made, work FPdc around next dc, sc in next dc; repeat from ★ across.

Row 9: Ch 3, turn; dc in next st and in each st across.

Row 10: Ch 1, turn; sc in first 2 dc, working in **front** of previous row, work FPdc around FPdc one row **below** each of next 3 dc, skip each dc behind FPdc just made, ★ sc in next 3 dc, working in **front** of previous row, work FPdc around FPdc one row **below** each of next 3 dc, skip each dc behind FPdc just made; repeat from ★ across to last 2 dc, sc in last 2 dc.

Row 11: Ch 3, turn; dc in next st and in each st across.

Row 12: Ch 1, turn; sc in first 3 dc, working in **front** of previous row, work FPdc around FPdc one row **below** next dc, skip dc behind FPdc just made, ★ sc in next 5 dc, working in **front** of previous row, work FPdc around FPdc one row **below** next dc, skip dc behind FPdc just made; repeat from ★ across to last 3 dc, sc in last 3 dc.

Repeat Rows 3-12 for pattern.

Beehive

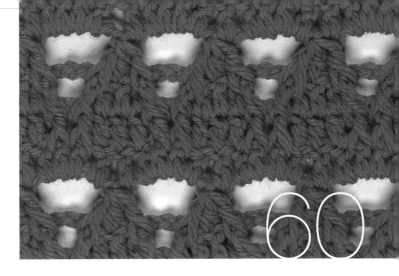

Chain a multiple of 6 + 9 chs.

Row 1 (Wrong side): Dc in fourth ch from hook **(3 skipped chs count as first dc)** and in next 4 chs, ch 1, ★ skip next ch, dc in next 5 chs, ch 1; repeat from ★ across to last 7 chs, skip next ch, dc in last 6 chs.

Note: Loop a short piece of yarn around the **back** of any stitch on Row 1 to mark **right** side.

To work Front Post double crochet (abbreviated FPdc), YO, insert hook from **front** to **back** around post of dc indicated *(Fig. 1, page 79)*, YO and pull up a loop (3 loops on hook), (YO and draw through 2 loops on hook) twice.

Row 2: Ch 3 **(counts as first dc, now and throughout)**, turn; work FPdc around next dc, dc in next 3 dc, work FPdc around next dc, ★ ch 1, work FPdc around next dc, dc in next 3 dc, work FPdc around next dc; repeat from ★ across to last dc, dc in last dc.

To work Left Back Post double crochet decrease (abbreviated Left BPdc decrease), YO, insert hook from **back** to **front** around post of next FPdc *(Fig. 1, page 79)*, YO and pull up a loop, YO and draw through 2 loops on hook, YO, insert hook in next dc, YO and pull up a loop, YO and draw through 2 loops on hook, YO and draw through all 3 loops on hook.

To work Right Back Post double crochet decrease (abbreviated Right BPdc decrease), YO, insert hook in next dc, YO and pull up a loop, YO and draw through 2 loops on hook, YO, insert hook from **back** to **front** around post of next FPdc *(Fig. 1, page 79)*, YO and pull up a loop, YO and draw through 2 loops on hook, YO and draw through all 3 loops on hook.

Row 3: Ch 4 **(counts as first dc plus ch 1, now and throughout)**, turn; work Left BPdc decrease, dc in next dc, work Right BPdc decrease, ★ ch 3, work Left BPdc decrease, dc in next dc, work Right BPdc decrease; repeat from ★ across to last dc, ch 1, dc in last dc.

To work Front Post double crochet decrease (abbreviated FPdc decrease), † YO, insert hook from **front** to **back** around post of next st *(Fig. 1, page 79)*, YO and pull up a loop, YO and draw through 2 loops on hook †, YO, insert hook in next dc, YO and pull up a loop, YO and draw through 2 loops on hook, repeat from † to † once, YO and draw through all 4 loops on hook.

Row 4: Ch 5 **(counts as first dc plus ch 2)**, turn; work FPdc decrease, (ch 5, work FPdc decrease) across to last dc, ch 2, dc in last dc.

Row 5: Ch 3, turn; 2 dc in next ch-2 sp, dc in next st, ★ (2 dc, ch 1, 2 dc) in next ch-5 sp, dc in next st; repeat from ★ across to last ch-2 sp, 2 dc in last ch-2 sp, dc in last dc.

Row 6: Ch 3, turn; work FPdc around next dc, dc in next 3 dc, work FPdc around next dc, ★ ch 1, work FPdc around next dc, dc in next 3 dc, work FPdc around next dc; repeat from ★ across to last dc, dc in last dc.

Row 7: Ch 4, turn; work Left BPdc decrease, dc in next dc, work Right BPdc decrease, ★ ch 3, work Left BPdc decrease, dc in next dc, work Right BPdc decrease; repeat from ★ across to last dc, ch 1, dc in last dc.

Repeat Rows 4-7 for pattern.

41

Lace Diamonds

Chain a multiple of 8 + 2 chs.

Row 1 (Right side)**:** Sc in second ch from hook, ★ ch 1, skip next 3 chs, (2 dc, ch 3, 2 dc) in next ch, ch 1, skip next 3 chs, sc in next ch; repeat from ★ across.

Note: Loop a short piece of yarn around any stitch to mark Row 1 as **right** side.

To work Front Post double crochet 2 together *(abbreviated FPdc2tog)* (uses next 2 dc), ★ YO, insert hook from **front** to **back** around post of **next** dc *(Fig. 1, page 79)*, YO and pull up a loop, YO and draw through 2 loops on hook; repeat from ★ once **more**, YO and draw through all 3 loops on hook (**counts as one decrease**).

To work Front Post double crochet 4 together *(abbreviated FPdc4tog)* (uses next 4 dc), ★ YO, insert hook from **front** to **back** around post of **next** dc *(Fig. 1, page 79)*, YO and pull up a loop, YO and draw through 2 loops on hook; repeat from ★ 3 times **more**, YO and draw through all 5 loops on hook (**counts as one decrease**).

Row 2: Ch 3 (**counts as first dc, now and throughout**), turn; work FPdc2tog, ch 3, sc in next ch-3 sp, ch 3, ★ work FPdc4tog, ch 3, sc in next ch-3 sp, ch 3; repeat from ★ across to last 3 sts, work FPdc2tog, dc in last sc.

Row 3: Ch 3, turn; 2 dc in next decrease, ch 1, skip next ch-3 sp, sc in next sc, ch 1, ★ skip next 2 chs, (2 dc, ch 3, 2 dc) in next ch, ch 1, skip next ch-3 sp, sc in next sc, ch 1; repeat from ★ across to last ch-3 sp, skip last ch-3 sp, 2 dc in next decrease, dc in last dc.

Row 4: Ch 1, turn; sc in first dc, ch 3, work FPdc4tog, ch 3, ★ sc in next ch-3 sp, ch 3, work FPdc4tog, ch 3; repeat from ★ across to last dc, sc in last dc.

Row 5: Ch 1, turn; sc in first sc, ★ ch 1, skip next 2 chs, (2 dc, ch 3, 2 dc) in next ch, ch 1, skip next ch-3 sp, sc in next sc; repeat from ★ across.

Repeat Rows 2-5 for pattern.

Double-Up Stitch

Chain a multiple of 12 + 3 chs.

Row 1 (Wrong side)**:** Dc in fourth ch from hook (**3 skipped chs count as first dc**) and in next ch, ch 1, skip next 3 chs, 5 dc in next ch, ch 1, ★ skip next 3 chs, dc in next 5 chs, ch 1, skip next 3 chs, 5 dc in next ch, ch 1; repeat from ★ across to last 6 chs, skip next 3 chs, dc in last 3 chs.

Note: Loop a short piece of yarn around the **back** of any stitch on Row 1 to mark **right** side.

To work Front Post treble crochet (abbreviated FPtr), YO twice, insert hook from **front** to **back** around post of dc indicated (*Fig. 1, page 79*), YO and pull up a loop (4 loops on hook), (YO and draw through 2 loops on hook) 3 times.

Row 2: Ch 3 (**counts as first dc, now and throughout**), turn; dc in next 2 dc, ch 1, dc in next dc, skip next 2 dc, work FPtr around next dc, ch 1, working in **front** of FPtr just made, work FPtr around first skipped dc, dc in next dc, ch 1, ★ dc in next 5 dc, ch 1, dc in next dc, skip next 2 dc, work FPtr around next dc, ch 1, working in **front** of FPtr just made, work FPtr around first skipped dc, dc in next dc, ch 1; repeat from ★ across to last 3 dc, dc in last 3 dc.

Row 3: Ch 3, turn; dc in next 2 dc, ch 1, skip next ch-1 sp, 5 dc in next ch-1 sp, ch 1, ★ skip next ch-1 sp, dc in next 5 dc, ch 1, skip next ch-1 sp, 5 dc in next ch-1 sp, ch 1; repeat from ★ across to last ch-1 sp, skip last ch-1 sp, dc in last 3 dc.

Repeat Rows 2 and 3 for pattern.

Berry Stitch

Chain a multiple of 6 + 3 chs.

Row 1 (Right side)**:** 4 Dc in sixth ch from hook (**5 skipped chs count as first dc and 2 skipped chs**), skip next 2 chs, dc in next ch, ★ skip next 2 chs, 4 dc in next ch, skip next 2 chs, dc in next ch; repeat from ★ across.

Note: Loop a short piece of yarn around any stitch to mark Row 1 as **right** side.

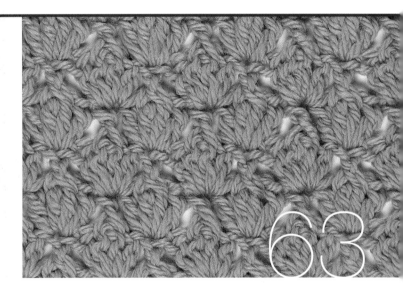

To work Back Post double crochet (abbreviated BPdc) (uses next 2 dc), YO, insert hook from **back** to **front** around post of next 2 dc as if they were one st (*Fig. 1, page 79*), YO and pull up a loop (3 loops on hook), (YO and draw through 2 loops on hook) twice.

Row 2: Ch 3 (**counts as first dc, now and throughout**), turn; 2 dc in first dc, skip next dc, work BPdc, ★ skip next dc, 4 dc in next dc, skip next dc, work BPdc; repeat from ★ across to last 2 dc, skip next dc, 3 dc in last dc.

To work Front Post double crochet (abbreviated FPdc) (uses next 2 dc), YO, insert hook from **front** to **back** around post of next 2 dc as if they were one st (*Fig. 1, page 79*), YO and pull up a loop (3 loops on hook), (YO and draw through 2 loops on hook) twice.

Row 3: Ch 3, turn; skip next 2 dc, 4 dc in next BPdc, ★ skip next dc, work FPdc, skip next dc, 4 dc in next BPdc; repeat from ★ across to last 3 dc, skip next 2 dc, dc in last dc.

Row 4: Ch 3, turn; 2 dc in first dc, skip next dc, work BPdc, ★ skip next dc, 4 dc in next FPdc, skip next dc, work BPdc; repeat from ★ across to last 2 dc, skip next dc, 3 dc in last dc.

Repeat Rows 3 and 4 for pattern.

Delicado

Chain a multiple of 4 + 3 chs.

Row 1 (Right side)**:** Dc in fourth ch from hook (**3 skipped chs count as first dc**) and in each ch across.

Note: Loop a short piece of yarn around any stitch to mark Row 1 as **right** side.

To work Front Post decrease (abbreviated FP decrease) (uses next 3 dc), ★ YO, insert hook from **front** to **back** around post of **next** dc *(Fig. 1, page 79)*, YO and pull up a loop, YO and draw through 2 loops on hook; repeat from ★ 2 times **more**, YO and draw through all 4 loops on hook.

Row 2: Ch 4 (**counts as first dc plus ch 1**), turn; work FP decrease, ch 1, dc in next dc, ★ ch 1, work FP decrease, ch 1, dc in next dc; repeat from ★ across.

Row 3: Ch 3 (**counts as first dc**), turn; dc in each ch-1 sp and in each st across.

Repeat Rows 2 and 3 for pattern.

Faux Cable

Chain a multiple of 5 + 4 chs.

Row 1 (Right side)**:** Hdc in third ch from hook (**2 skipped chs count as first hdc**) and in each ch across.

Note: Loop a short piece of yarn around any stitch to mark Row 1 as **right** side.

Row 2: Ch 2 (**counts as first hdc, now and throughout**), turn; hdc in next hdc and in each hdc across.

To work Front Post treble crochet (abbreviated FPtr), YO twice, working in **front** of previous row *(Fig. 2, page 80)*, insert hook from **front** to **back** around post of hdc indicated *(Fig. 1, page 79)*, YO and pull up a loop (4 loops on hook), (YO and draw through 2 loops on hook) 3 times. Skip hdc behind FPtr.

Row 3: Ch 2, turn; hdc in next 2 hdc, ★ skip next hdc, work FPtr around hdc one row **below** next hdc, hdc in next 4 hdc; repeat from ★ across.

Row 4: Ch 2, turn; hdc in next st and in each st across.

Repeat Rows 3 and 4 for pattern.

Twister

Chain a multiple of 8 + 3 chs.

Row 1 (Wrong side)**:** Dc in fourth ch from hook
(**3 skipped chs count as first dc**) and in each ch across.

Note: Loop a short piece of yarn around the **back** of any
stitch on Row 1 to mark **right** side.

To work Front Post double crochet (abbreviated FPdc),
YO, insert hook from **front** to **back** around post of
st indicated *(Fig. 1, page 79)*, YO and pull up a loop
(3 loops on hook), (YO and draw through 2 loops on
hook) twice.

Row 2: Ch 1, turn; sc in first 3 dc, skip next 2 dc, work
FPdc around next dc, skip next dc from last sc made,
sc in next dc, working in **front** of last FPdc made, work
FPdc around first skipped dc, ★ skip next dc from last sc
made, sc in next 5 dc, skip next 2 dc, work FPdc around
next dc, skip next dc from last sc made, sc in next dc,
working in **front** of last FPdc made, work FPdc around
first skipped dc; repeat from ★ across to last 4 dc, skip
next dc from last sc made, sc in last 3 dc.

Row 3: Ch 3 (**counts as first dc, now and throughout**),
turn; dc in next st and in each st across.

Row 4: Ch 1, turn; sc in first 3 dc, working in **front** of
previous row *(Fig. 2, page 80)*, work FPdc around FPdc
one row **below** next dc, skip dc behind FPdc, sc in next
dc, working in **front** of previous row, work FPdc around
FPdc one row **below** next dc, skip dc behind FPdc,
★ sc in next 5 dc, working in **front** of previous row,
work FPdc around FPdc one row **below** next dc, skip dc
behind FPdc, sc in next dc, working in **front** of previous
row, work FPdc around FPdc one row **below** next dc,
skip dc behind FPdc; repeat from ★ across to last 3 dc,
sc in last 3 dc.

Row 5: Ch 3, turn; dc in next st and in each st across.

Row 6: Ch 1, turn; sc in first 3 dc, skip next 2 dc,
working in **front** of previous row, work FPdc around
FPdc one row **below** next dc, skip next dc from last sc
made, sc in next dc, working in **front** of previous row,
work FPdc around FPdc one row **below** first skipped dc,
skip next dc from last sc made, ★ sc in next 5 dc, skip
next 2 dc, working in **front** of previous row, work FPdc
around FPdc one row **below** next dc, skip next dc from
last sc made, sc in next dc, working in **front** of previous
row, work FPdc around FPdc one row **below** first
skipped dc, skip next dc from last sc made; repeat from
★ across to last 3 dc, sc in last 3 dc.

Row 7: Ch 3, turn; dc in next st and in each st across.

Repeat Rows 4-7 for pattern.

Spring Blooms

Chain a multiple of 10 + 12 chs.

Row 1 (Right side)**:** Sc in second ch from hook and in each ch across.

Note: Loop a short piece of yarn around any stitch to mark Row 1 as **right** side.

Row 2: Ch 1, turn; sc in each sc across.

To work Front Post double crochet (abbreviated FPdc), YO, working in **front** of previous row(s) *(Fig. 2, page 80)*, insert hook from **front** to **back** around post of st indicated *(Fig. 1, page 79)*, YO and pull up a loop (3 loops on hook), (YO and draw through 2 loops on hook) twice. Skip sc behind FPdc.

Row 3: Ch 1, turn; sc in first 5 sc, work FPdc around sc one row **below** next sc, ★ sc in next 9 sc, work FPdc around sc one row **below** next sc; repeat from ★ across to last 5 sc, sc in last 5 sc.

Row 4: Ch 1, turn; sc in each st across.

Row 5: Ch 1, turn; sc in first 5 sc, work FPdc around FPdc one row **below** next sc, ★ sc in next 9 sc, work FPdc around FPdc one row **below** next sc; repeat from ★ across to last 5 sc, sc in last 5 sc.

Row 6: Ch 1, turn; sc in each st across.

To work Front Post treble crochet (abbreviated FPtr), YO twice, working in **front** of previous row *(Fig. 2, page 80)*, insert hook from **front** to **back** around post of sc indicated *(Fig. 1, page 79)*, YO and pull up a loop (4 loops on hook), (YO and draw through 2 loops on hook) 3 times. Skip sc behind FPtr.

Row 7: Ch 1, turn; sc in first 2 sc, † work FPtr around sc **before** next FPdc 5 rows **below**, sc in next 2 sc, work FPdc around FPdc one row **below** next sc, sc in next 2 sc, work FPtr around sc **after** FPdc 5 rows **below** †, sc in next 3 sc, repeat from † to † across to last 2 sc, sc in last 2 sc.

Row 8: Ch 1, turn; sc in each st across.

To work Popcorn (uses one sc), 5 hdc in sc indicated, drop loop from hook, insert hook from **front** to **back** in first hdc of 5-hdc group, hook dropped loop and draw through st.

Row 9: Ch 1, turn; sc in first 5 sc, work Popcorn in next sc, (sc in next 9 sc, work Popcorn in next sc) across to last 5 sc, sc in last 5 sc.

Row 10: Ch 1, turn; sc in each st across.

Row 11: Ch 1, turn; sc in first 10 sc, work FPdc around sc 2 rows **below** next sc, ★ sc in next 9 sc, work FPdc around sc 2 rows **below** next sc; repeat from ★ across to last 10 sc, sc in last 10 sc.

Row 12: Ch 1, turn; sc in each st across.

Row 13: Ch 1, turn; sc in first 10 sc, work FPdc around FPdc one row **below** next sc, ★ sc in next 9 sc, work FPdc around FPdc one row **below** next sc; repeat from ★ across to last 10 sc, sc in last 10 sc.

Row 14: Ch 1, turn; sc in each st across.

Row 15: Ch 1, turn; sc in first 7 sc, † work FPtr around sc **before** next FPdc 5 rows **below**, sc in next 2 sc, work FPdc around FPdc one row **below** next sc, sc in next 2 sc, work FPtr around sc **after** FPdc 5 rows **below** †, sc in next 3 sc, repeat from † to † across to last 7 sc, sc in last 7 sc.

Row 16: Ch 1, turn; sc in each st across.

Row 17: Ch 1, turn; sc in first 10 sc, work Popcorn in next sc, (sc in next 9 sc, work Popcorn in next sc) across to last 10 sc, sc in last 10 sc.

Row 18: Ch 1, turn; sc in each st across.

Row 19: Ch 1, turn; sc in first 5 sc, work FPdc around sc 2 rows **below** next sc, ★ sc in next 9 sc, work FPdc around sc 2 rows **below** next sc; repeat from ★ across to last 5 sc, sc in last 5 sc.

Repeat Rows 4-19 for pattern.

Crossed Stripes

Note: Uses MC, Color A, and Color B in the following sequence: One row MC, ★ 2 rows **each** Color A, MC, Color B, MC; repeat from ★ for stripe sequence.

With MC, chain a multiple of 6 + 3 chs.

Row 1 (Wrong side)**:** Sc in second ch from hook and in each ch across; finish off.

Note: Loop a short piece of yarn around the **back** of any stitch on Row 1 to mark **right** side.

Row 2: With **right** side facing, join Color A with sc in first sc *(see Joining With Sc, page 79)*; sc in next sc and in each sc across.

Row 3: Ch 1, turn; sc in each sc across; finish off.

To work Front Post double crochet *(abbreviated FPdc),* YO, working in **front** of previous rows *(Fig. 2, page 80),* insert hook from **front** to **back** around post of sc indicated *(Fig. 1, page 79),* YO and pull up a loop (3 loops on hook), (YO and draw through 2 loops on hook) twice. Skip sc behind FPdc.

Row 4: With **right** side facing, join MC with sc in first sc; work FPdc around fourth sc 3 rows **below**, sc in next 4 sc on previous row, work FPdc around next sc 3 rows **below** (after last FPdc made), ★ skip next 4 sc 3 rows **below**, work FPdc around next sc, sc in next 4 sc on previous row, work FPdc around next sc 3 rows **below**; repeat from ★ across to last sc on previous row, sc in last sc.

Row 5: Ch 1, turn; sc in each st across; finish off.

Row 6: With **right** side facing, join Color B with sc in first sc; sc in next sc and in each sc across.

Row 7: Ch 1, turn; sc in each sc across; finish off.

Row 8: With **right** side facing, join MC with sc in first sc; sc in next 2 sc, work FPdc around second sc 3 rows **below**, skip next 4 sc 3 rows **below**, work FPdc around next sc, ★ sc in next 4 sc on previous row, work FPdc around next sc 3 rows **below**, skip next 4 sc 3 rows **below**, work FPdc around next sc; repeat from ★ across to last 3 sc on previous row, sc in last 3 sc.

Row 9: Ch 1, turn; sc in each st across; finish off.

Row 10: With **right** side facing, join Color A with sc in first sc; sc in next sc and in each sc across.

Row 11: Ch 1, turn; sc in each sc across; finish off.

Repeat Rows 4-11 for pattern.

Raised Diamonds

Chain a multiple of 6 + 5 chs.

To treble crochet (abbreviated tr), YO twice, insert hook in st indicated, YO and pull up a loop (4 loops on hook), (YO and draw through 2 loops on hook) 3 times.

Row 1 (Wrong side): 3 Tr in eighth ch from hook **(7 skipped chs count as first tr plus ch 1 and 2 skipped chs)**, ch 1, skip next 2 chs, tr in next ch, ★ ch 1, skip next 2 chs, 3 tr in next ch, ch 1, skip next 2 chs, tr in next ch; repeat from ★ across.

Note: Loop a short piece of yarn around the **back** of any stitch on Row 1 to mark **right** side.

To work Front Post treble crochet Cluster (abbreviated FPtr Cluster) (uses next 3 tr), ★ YO twice, insert hook from **front** to **back** around post of **next** tr *(Fig. 1, page 79)*, YO and pull up a loop, (YO and draw through 2 loops on hook) twice; repeat from ★ 2 times **more**, YO and draw through all 4 loops on hook.

Row 2: Ch 6 **(counts as first tr plus ch 2, now and throughout)**, turn; work FPtr Cluster, ch 2, tr in next tr, ★ ch 2, work FPtr Cluster, ch 2, tr in next tr; repeat from ★ across.

Row 3: Ch 4 **(counts as first tr, now and throughout)**, turn; tr in first tr, ch 1, tr in next FPtr Cluster, ch 1, ★ 3 tr in next tr, ch 1, tr in next FPtr Cluster, ch 1; repeat from ★ across to last tr, 2 tr in last tr.

Row 4: Ch 4, turn; tr in first tr, ch 1, skip next tr, tr in next tr, ★ ch 2, work FPtr Cluster, ch 2, tr in next tr; repeat from ★ across to last 2 tr, ch 1, skip next tr, 2 tr in last tr.

Row 5: Ch 5 **(counts as first tr plus ch 1)**, turn; skip next tr, 3 tr in next tr, ch 1, ★ tr in next FPtr Cluster, ch 1, 3 tr in next tr, ch 1; repeat from ★ across to last 2 tr, skip next tr, tr in last tr.

Repeat Rows 2-5 for pattern.

Triangles

Chain a multiple of 4 + 2 chs.

Row 1 (Wrong side): Sc in second ch from hook and in each ch across.

Note: Loop a short piece of yarn around the **back** of any stitch on Row 1 to mark **right** side.

Row 2: Ch 3 **(counts as first dc, now and throughout)**, turn; ★ skip next sc, 3 dc in next sc, skip next sc, dc in next sc; repeat from ★ across.

Row 3: Ch 1, turn; sc in each dc across.

To work Front Post double crochet (abbreviated FPdc), working in **front** of previous row *(Fig. 2, page 80)*, YO, insert hook from **front** to **back** around post of dc indicated *(Fig. 1, page 79)*, YO and pull up a loop (3 loops on hook), (YO and draw through 2 loops on hook) twice.

Row 4: Ch 3, turn; dc in first sc, skip next sc, dc in next sc, ★ skip next sc, work 3 FPdc around dc one row **below** next sc, skip next 3 sc from last dc made, dc in next sc; repeat from ★ across to last 2 sc, skip next sc, 2 dc in last sc.

Row 5: Ch 1, turn; sc in each st across.

Row 6: Ch 3, turn; skip next sc, work 3 FPdc around dc one row **below** next sc, ★ skip next 3 sc from last dc made, dc in next sc, skip next sc, work 3 FPdc around dc one row **below** next sc; repeat from ★ across to last 4 sc, skip next 3 sc from last dc made, dc in last sc.

Row 7: Ch 1, turn; sc in each st across.

Repeat Rows 4-7 for pattern.

Lace Shells

Chain a multiple of 8 + 2 chs.

To work Picot, ch 3, slip st in third ch from hook.

Row 1 (Right side): Sc in second ch from hook, ★ skip next 3 chs, dc in next ch, (work Picot, dc in same st) 6 times, skip next 3 chs, sc in next ch; repeat from ★ across.

Note: Loop a short piece of yarn around any stitch to mark Row 1 as **right** side.

To work Front Post single crochet (abbreviated FPsc), insert hook from **front** to **back** around post of dc indicated *(Fig. 1, page 79)*, YO and pull up a loop, YO and draw through both loops on hook.

To work Front Post half double crochet (abbreviated FPhdc), YO, insert hook from **front** to **back** around post of dc indicated *(Fig. 1, page 79)*, YO and pull up a loop, YO and draw through all 3 loops on hook.

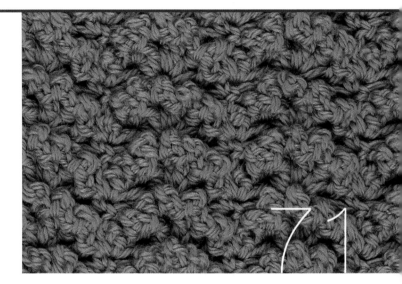

Row 2: Ch 4 (**counts as first dc plus ch 1**), skip next dc, work FPhdc around next dc, ch 1, skip next dc, work FPsc around next dc, ch 1, skip next dc, work FPhdc around next dc, ch 1, skip next dc, dc in next sc, ★ ch 1, skip next dc, work FPhdc around next dc, ch 1, skip next dc, work FPsc around next dc, ch 1, skip next dc, work FPhdc around next dc, ch 1, skip next dc, dc in next sc; repeat from ★ across.

Row 3: Ch 1, turn; sc in first dc, ★ skip next FPhdc, dc in next FPsc, (work Picot, dc in same st) 6 times, skip next FPhdc, sc in next dc; repeat from ★ across.

Repeat Rows 2 and 3 for pattern.

Sharp Chevrons

Chain a multiple of 16 + 2 chs.

Row 1 (Wrong side)**:** YO, insert hook in third ch from hook, YO and pull up a loop, YO and draw through 2 loops on hook, YO, insert hook in next ch, YO and pull up a loop, YO and draw through 2 loops on hook, YO and draw through all 3 loops on hook, dc in next 5 chs, (2 dc, ch 1, 2 dc) in next ch, dc in next 5 chs, ★ [YO, insert hook in **next** ch, YO and pull up a loop, YO and draw through 2 loops on hook] 5 times, YO and draw through all 6 loops on hook, dc in next 5 chs, (2 dc, ch 1, 2 dc) in next ch, dc in next 5 chs; repeat from ★ across to last 3 chs, [YO, insert hook in **next** ch, YO and pull up a loop, YO and draw through 2 loops on hook] 3 times, YO and draw through all 4 loops on hook.

Note: Loop a short piece of yarn around the **back** of any stitch on Row 1 to mark **right** side.

To work Front Post double crochet 2 together *(abbreviated FPdc2tog) (uses next 2 sts),* ★ YO, insert hook from **front** to **back** around post of **next** st *(Fig. 1, page 79)*, YO and pull up a loop, YO and draw through 2 loops on hook; repeat from ★ once **more**, YO and draw through all 3 loops on hook.

To work Front Post double crochet 3 together *(abbreviated FPdc3tog) (uses next 3 sts),* ★ YO, insert hook from **front** to **back** around post of **next** st *(Fig. 1, page 79)*, YO and pull up a loop, YO and draw through 2 loops on hook; repeat from ★ 2 times **more**, YO and draw through all 4 loops on hook.

To work Front Post double crochet 5 together *(abbreviated FPdc5tog) (uses next 5 sts),* ★ YO, insert hook from **front** to **back** around post of **next** st *(Fig. 1, page 79)*, YO and pull up a loop, YO and draw through 2 loops on hook; repeat from ★ 4 times **more**, YO and draw through all 6 loops on hook.

To work Front Post double crochet *(abbreviated FPdc),* YO, insert hook from **front** to **back** around post of st indicated *(Fig. 1, page 79)*, YO and pull up a loop (3 loops on hook), (YO and draw through 2 loops on hook) twice.

Row 2: Ch 2, turn; skip first st, work FPdc2tog, work FPdc around each of next 5 dc, (2 dc, ch 1, 2 dc) in next ch-1 sp, work FPdc around each of next 5 dc, ★ work FPdc5tog, work FPdc around each of next 5 dc, (2 dc, ch 1, 2 dc) in next ch-1 sp, work FPdc around each of next 5 dc; repeat from ★ across to last 3 sts, work FPdc3tog.

To work Back Post double crochet 2 together *(abbreviated BPdc2tog) (uses next 2 sts),* ★ YO, insert hook from **back** to **front** around post of **next** st *(Fig. 1, page 79)*, YO and pull up a loop, YO and draw through 2 loops on hook; repeat from ★ once **more**, YO and draw through all 3 loops on hook.

To work Back Post double crochet 3 together *(abbreviated BPdc3tog) (uses next 3 sts),* ★ YO, insert hook from **back** to **front** around post of **next** st *(Fig. 1, page 79)*, YO and pull up a loop, YO and draw through 2 loops on hook; repeat from ★ 2 times **more**, YO and draw through all 4 loops on hook.

To work Back Post double crochet 5 together *(abbreviated BPdc5tog) (uses next 5 sts),* ★ YO, insert hook from **back** to **front** around post of **next** st *(Fig. 1, page 79)*, YO and pull up a loop, YO and draw through 2 loops on hook; repeat from ★ 4 times **more**, YO and draw through all 6 loops on hook.

To work Back Post double crochet (*abbreviated BPdc*), YO, insert hook from **front** to **back** around post of st indicated (*Fig. 1, page 79*), YO and pull up a loop (3 loops on hook), (YO and draw through 2 loops on hook) twice.

Row 3: Ch 2, turn; skip first st, work BPdc2tog, work BPdc around each of next 5 sts, (2 dc, ch 1, 2 dc) in next ch-1 sp, work BPdc around each of next 5 sts, ★ work BPdc5tog, work BPdc around each of next 5 sts, (2 dc, ch 1, 2 dc) in next ch-1 sp, work BPdc around each of next 5 sts; repeat from ★ across to last 3 sts, work BPdc3tog.

Row 4: Ch 2, turn; skip first st, work FPdc2tog, work FPdc around each of next 5 sts, (2 dc, ch 1, 2 dc) in next ch-1 sp, work FPdc around each of next 5 sts, ★ work FPdc5tog, work FPdc around each of next 5 sts, (2 dc, ch 1, 2 dc) in next ch-1 sp, work FPdc around each of next 5 sts; repeat from ★ across to last 3 sts, work FPdc3tog.

Repeat Rows 3 and 4 for pattern.

La Petite

Chain a multiple of 7 + 2 chs.

Row 1 (Right side)**:** Dc in fourth ch from hook (**3 skipped chs count as first dc**), ch 1, skip next ch, dc in next ch, ch 1, ★ skip next ch, dc in next 4 chs, ch 1, skip next ch, dc in next ch, ch 1; repeat from ★ across to last 3 chs, skip next ch, dc in last 2 chs.

Note: Loop a short piece of yarn around any stitch to mark Row 1 as **right** side.

Row 2: Ch 1, turn; sc in first dc, skip next dc, dc in next dc, (ch 1, dc in same st) twice, ★ skip next dc, sc in next 2 dc, skip next dc, dc in next dc, (ch 1, dc in same st) twice; repeat from ★ across to last 2 dc, skip next dc, sc in last dc.

To work Front Post double crochet (*abbreviated FPdc*), YO, insert hook from **front** to **back** around post of dc indicated (*Fig. 1, page 79*), YO and pull up a loop (3 loops on hook), (YO and draw through 2 loops on hook) twice.

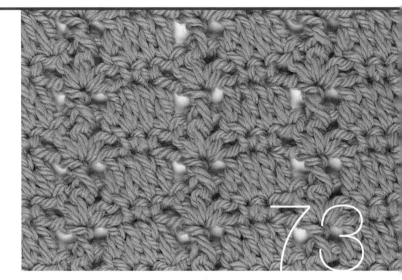

Row 3: Ch 3 (**counts as first dc**), turn; dc in next dc, ch 1, work FPdc around next dc, ch 1, dc in next dc, ★ dc in next 2 sc and in next dc, ch 1, work FPdc around next dc, ch 1, dc in next dc; repeat from ★ across to last sc, dc in last sc.

Row 4: Ch 1, turn; sc in first dc, skip next dc, dc in next FPdc, (ch 1, dc in same st) twice, ★ skip next dc, sc in next 2 dc, skip next dc, dc in next FPdc, (ch 1, dc in same st) twice; repeat from ★ across to last 2 dc, skip next dc, sc in last dc.

Repeat Rows 3 and 4 for pattern.

Posted V's

Chain a multiple of 3 + 4 chs.

Row 1 (Wrong side)**:** Dc in fourth ch from hook
(3 skipped chs count as first dc) and in each ch across.

Note: Loop a short piece of yarn around the **back** of any
stitch on Row 1 to mark **right** side.

Row 2: Ch 3 **(counts as first dc, now and throughout)**,
turn; skip next dc, (dc, ch 1, dc) in next dc, ★ skip next
2 dc, (dc, ch 1, dc) in next dc; repeat from ★ across to
last 2 dc, skip next dc, dc in last dc.

To work Back Post double crochet (abbreviated BPdc),
YO, insert hook from **back** to **front** around post of
dc indicated *(Fig. 1, page 79)*, YO and pull up a loop
(3 loops on hook), (YO and draw through 2 loops on
hook) twice.

Row 3: Ch 3, turn; work BPdc around next dc, dc in
next ch-1 sp, ★ work BPdc around each of next 2 dc, dc
in next ch-1 sp; repeat from ★ across to last 2 dc, work
BPdc around next dc, dc in last dc.

To work Front Post double crochet (abbreviated FPdc),
YO, insert hook from **front** to **back** around post of
dc indicated *(Fig. 1, page 79)*, YO and pull up a loop
(3 loops on hook), (YO and draw through 2 loops on
hook) twice.

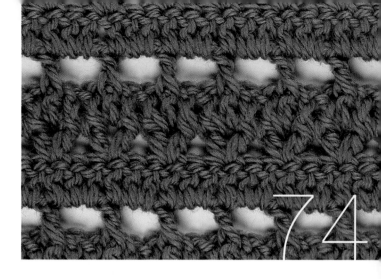

Row 4: Ch 4 **(counts as first dc plus ch 1)**, turn; skip
next BPdc, work FPdc around next dc, ★ ch 2, skip
next 2 BPdc, work FPdc around next dc; repeat from
★ across to last 2 sts, ch 1, skip next BPdc, dc in last dc.

Row 5: Ch 3, turn; dc in next ch-1 sp and in next FPdc,
(2 dc in next ch-2 sp, dc in next FPdc) across to last
ch-1 sp, dc in last ch-1 sp and in last dc.

Row 6: Ch 3, turn; skip next dc, (dc, ch 1, dc) in next dc,
★ skip next 2 dc, (dc, ch 1, dc) in next dc; repeat from
★ across to last 2 dc, skip next dc, dc in last dc.

Row 7: Ch 3, turn; work BPdc around next dc, dc in
next ch-1 sp, ★ work BPdc around each of next 2 dc,
dc in next ch-1 sp; repeat from ★ across to last 2 dc, work
BPdc around next dc, dc in last dc.

Repeat Rows 4-7 for pattern.

Simple Bands

Chain a multiple of 12 + 13 chs.

Row 1 (Wrong side)**:** Dc in fourth ch from hook (**3 skipped chs count as first dc**) and in next ch, ch 1, skip next 2 chs, (dc, ch 1) twice in next ch, ★ skip next 2 chs, dc in next 7 chs, ch 1, skip next 2 chs, (dc, ch 1) twice in next ch; repeat from ★ across to last 5 chs, skip next 2 chs, dc in last 3 chs.

Note: Loop a short piece of yarn around the **back** of any stitch on Row 1 to mark **right** side.

To work Front Post double crochet (*abbreviated FPdc*), YO, insert hook from **front** to **back** around post of st indicated (***Fig. 1, page 79***), YO and pull up a loop (3 loops on hook), (YO and draw through 2 loops on hook) twice.

To decrease (uses next 2 dc), ★ YO, insert hook in **next** dc, YO and pull up a loop, YO and draw through 2 loops on hook; repeat from ★ once **more**, YO and draw through all 3 loops on hook (**counts as one dc**).

Row 2: Ch 3 (**counts as first dc, now and throughout**), turn; dc in next dc, work FPdc around next dc, ch 2, decrease, ch 2, work FPdc around next dc, ★ dc in next 5 dc, work FPdc around next dc, ch 2, decrease, ch 2, work FPdc around next dc; repeat from ★ across to last 2 dc, dc in last 2 dc.

To work Back Post double crochet (*abbreviated BPdc*), YO, insert hook from **back** to **front** around post of FPdc indicated (***Fig. 1, page 79***), YO and pull up a loop (3 loops on hook), (YO and draw through 2 loops on hook) twice.

Row 3: Ch 3, turn; dc in next dc, work BPdc around next FPdc, ch 1, (dc, ch 1) twice in next dc, work BPdc around next FPdc, ★ dc in next 5 dc, work BPdc around next FPdc, ch 1, (dc, ch 1) twice in next dc, work BPdc around next FPdc; repeat from ★ across to last 2 dc, dc in last 2 dc.

Row 4: Ch 3, turn; dc in next dc, work FPdc around next BPdc, ch 2, decrease, ch 2, work FPdc around next BPdc, ★ dc in next 5 dc, work FPdc around next BPdc, ch 2, decrease, ch 2, work FPdc around next BPdc; repeat from ★ across to last 2 dc, dc in last 2 dc.

Repeat Rows 3 and 4 for pattern.

Accent

Chain a multiple of 8 + 2 chs.

Row 1 (Right side): Sc in second ch from hook, ★ ch 2, skip next 2 chs, dc in next 3 chs, ch 2, skip next 2 chs, sc in next ch; repeat from ★ across.

Note: Loop a short piece of yarn around any stitch to mark Row 1 as **right** side.

Row 2: Ch 3 (**counts as first dc, now and throughout**), turn; ★ dc in next ch-2 sp, ch 2, skip next dc, sc in next dc, ch 2, dc in next ch-2 sp and in next sc; repeat from ★ across.

To work Front Post double crochet (abbreviated FPdc), YO, insert hook from **front** to **back** around post of dc indicated (*Fig. 1, page 79*), YO and pull up a loop (3 loops on hook), (YO and draw through 2 loops on hook) twice.

Row 3: Ch 3, turn; dc in next dc, ch 2, sc in next sc, ch 2, ★ dc in next dc, work FPdc around next dc, dc in next dc, ch 2, sc in next sc, ch 2; repeat from ★ across to last 2 dc, dc in last 2 dc.

Row 4: Ch 1, turn; sc in first dc, ★ ch 2, dc in next ch-2 sp and in next sc, dc in next ch-2 sp, ch 2, skip next dc, sc in next st; repeat from ★ across.

Row 5: Ch 1, turn; sc in first sc, ★ ch 2, dc in next dc, work FPdc around next dc, dc in next dc, ch 2, sc in next sc; repeat from ★ across.

Row 6: Ch 3, turn; ★ dc in next ch-2 sp, ch 2, skip next dc, sc in next FPdc, ch 2, dc in next ch-2 sp and in next sc; repeat from ★ across.

Repeat Rows 3-6 for pattern.

Dynamic
Diamonds

Chain a multiple of 14 + 2 chs.

Row 1 (Wrong side): Dc in fourth ch from hook (**3 skipped chs count as first dc**) and in each ch across.

Note: Loop a short piece of yarn around the **back** of any stitch on Row 1 to mark **right** side.

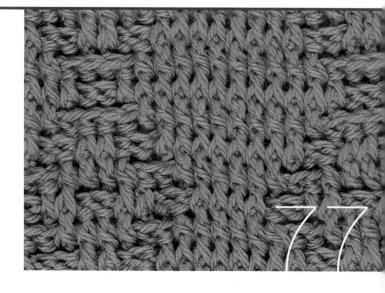

To work Front Post double crochet (abbreviated FPdc), YO, insert hook from **front** to **back** around post of st indicated *(Fig. 1, page 79)*, YO and pull up a loop (3 loops on hook), (YO and draw through 2 loops on hook) twice.

To work Back Post double crochet (abbreviated BPdc), YO, insert hook from **back** to **front** around post of st indicated *(Fig. 1, page 79)*, YO and pull up a loop (3 loops on hook), (YO and draw through 2 loops on hook) twice.

Row 2: Ch 2 (**counts as first hdc, now and throughout**), turn; work FPdc around each of next 5 dc, work BPdc around each of next 2 dc, ★ work FPdc around each of next 12 dc, work BPdc around each of next 2 dc; repeat from ★ across to last 6 sts, work FPdc around each of next 5 dc, hdc in last dc.

Row 3: Ch 2, turn; work BPdc around each of next 4 FPdc, work FPdc around each of next 4 sts, ★ work BPdc around each of next 10 FPdc, work FPdc around each of next 4 sts; repeat from ★ across to last 5 sts, work BPdc around each of next 4 FPdc, hdc in last hdc.

Row 4: Ch 2, turn; work FPdc around each of next 3 BPdc, work BPdc around each of next 2 sts, work FPdc around each of next 2 FPdc, work BPdc around each of next 2 sts, ★ work FPdc around each of next 8 BPdc, work BPdc around each of next 2 sts, work FPdc around each of next 2 FPdc, work BPdc around each of next 2 sts; repeat from ★ across to last 4 sts, work FPdc around each of next 3 BPdc, hdc in last hdc.

Row 5: Ch 2, turn; work BPdc around each of next 2 FPdc, work FPdc around each of next 2 sts, work BPdc around each of next 4 sts, work FPdc around each of next 2 sts, ★ work BPdc around each of next 6 FPdc, work FPdc around each of next 2 sts, work BPdc around each of next 4 sts, work FPdc around each of next 2 sts; repeat from ★ across to last 3 sts, work BPdc around each of next 2 FPdc, hdc in last hdc.

Row 6: Ch 2, turn; work FPdc around next BPdc, work BPdc around each of next 2 sts, (work FPdc around each of next 2 sts, work BPdc around each of next 2 sts) twice, ★ work FPdc around each of next 4 BPdc, work BPdc around each of next 2 sts, (work FPdc around each of next 2 sts, work BPdc around each of next 2 sts) twice; repeat from ★ across to last 2 sts, work FPdc around next BPdc, hdc in last hdc.

Row 7: Ch 2, turn; work BPdc around each of next 2 sts, work FPdc around each of next 2 sts, work BPdc around each of next 4 sts, work FPdc around each of next 2 sts, ★ work BPdc around each of next 6 sts, work FPdc around each of next 2 sts, work BPdc around each of next 4 sts, work FPdc around each of next 2 sts; repeat from ★ across to last 3 sts, work BPdc around each of next 2 sts, hdc in last hdc.

Row 8: Ch 2, turn; work FPdc around each of next 3 sts, work BPdc around each of next 2 sts, work FPdc around each of next 2 sts, work BPdc around each of next 2 sts, ★ work FPdc around each of next 8 sts, work BPdc around each of next 2 sts, work FPdc around each of next 2 sts, work BPdc around each of next 2 sts; repeat from ★ across to last 4 sts, work FPdc around each of next 3 sts, hdc in last hdc.

Row 9: Ch 2, turn; work BPdc around each of next 4 sts, work FPdc around each of next 4 sts, ★ work BPdc around each of next 10 sts, work FPdc around each of next 4 sts; repeat from ★ across to last 5 sts, work BPdc around each of next 4 sts, hdc in last hdc.

Row 10: Ch 2, turn; work FPdc around each of next 5 sts, work BPdc around each of next 2 sts, ★ work FPdc around each of next 12 sts, work BPdc around each of next 2 sts; repeat from ★ across to last 6 sts, work FPdc around each of next 5 sts, hdc in last hdc.

Repeat Rows 3-10 for pattern.

Hourglass I

Chain a multiple of 8 + 4 chs.

Row 1 (Wrong side)**:** Dc in fourth ch from hook (**3 skipped chs count as first dc**) and in each ch across.

Note: Loop a short piece of yarn around the **back** of any stitch on Row 1 to mark **right** side.

To work Front Post double crochet (*abbreviated FPdc*), YO, insert hook from **front** to **back** around post of st indicated (***Fig. 1, page 79***), YO and pull up a loop (3 loops on hook), (YO and draw through 2 loops on hook) twice.

Row 2: Ch 1, turn; sc in first dc, work FPdc around each of next 2 dc, sc in next 4 dc, ★ work FPdc around each of next 4 dc, sc in next 4 dc; repeat from ★ across to last 3 dc, work FPdc around each of next 2 dc, sc in last dc.

Row 3: Ch 3 (**counts as first dc, now and throughout**), turn; dc in next st and in each st across.

Row 4: Ch 1, turn; sc in first 3 dc, working in **front** of previous row (***Fig. 2, page 80***), work FPdc around each of first 4 FPdc 2 rows **below**, ★ skip next 4 dc from last sc made, sc in next 4 dc, work FPdc around each of next 4 FPdc 2 rows **below**; repeat from ★ across to last 7 dc, skip next 4 dc from last sc made, sc in last 3 dc.

Row 5: Ch 3, turn; dc in next st and in each st across.

Row 6: Ch 1, turn; sc in first 3 dc, working in **front** of previous row, work FPdc around each FPdc one row **below** next 4 dc, ★ skip next 4 dc from last sc made, sc in next 4 dc, work FPdc around each FPdc one row **below** next 4 dc; repeat from ★ across to last 7 dc, skip next 4 dc from last sc made, sc in last 3 dc.

Row 7: Ch 3, turn; dc in next st and in each st across.

Rows 8 and 9: Repeat Rows 6 and 7.

Row 10: Ch 1, turn; sc in first sc, working in **front** of previous row, work FPdc around each of next 2 FPdc 2 rows **below**, skip next 2 dc from last sc made, sc in next 4 dc, ★ work FPdc around each of next 4 FPdc 2 rows **below**, skip next 4 dc from last sc made, sc in next 4 dc; repeat from ★ across to last 3 dc, work FPdc around each of next 2 FPdc 2 rows **below**, skip next 2 dc from last sc made, sc in last dc.

Row 11: Ch 3, turn; dc in next st and in each st across.

Rows 12-15: Repeat Rows 10 and 11 twice.

Repeat Rows 4-15 for pattern.

Hourglass II

Chain a multiple of 6 + 3 chs.

Row 1 (Right side)**:** Sc in second ch from hook and in each ch across.

Note: Loop a short piece of yarn around any stitch to mark Row 1 as **right** side.

Row 2: Ch 1, turn; sc in each sc across.

To work Front Post double crochet (abbreviated FPdc), YO, working in **front** of previous row *(Fig. 2, page 80)*, insert hook from **front** to **back** around post of st indicated *(Fig. 1, page 79)*, YO and pull up a loop (3 loops on hook), (YO and draw through 2 loops on hook) twice. Skip sc behind FPdc.

Row 3: Ch 1, turn; sc in first 3 sc, work FPdc around sc one row **below** each of next 2 sc, ★ sc in next 4 sc, work FPdc around sc one row **below** each of next 2 sc; repeat from ★ across to last 3 sc, sc in last 3 sc.

Row 4: Ch 1, turn; sc in each st across.

Row 5: Ch 1, turn; sc in first sc, work FPdc around first FPdc 2 rows **below**, sc in next 4 sc, ★ work FPdc around each of next 2 FPdc 2 rows **below**, sc in next 4 sc; repeat from ★ across to last 2 sc, work FPdc around next FPdc 2 rows **below**, sc in last sc.

Rows 6-9: Repeat Rows 4 and 5 twice.

Row 10: Ch 1, turn; sc in each st across.

Row 11: Ch 1, turn; sc in first 3 sc, work FPdc around each of first 2 FPdc 2 rows **below**, ★ sc in next 4 sc, work FPdc around each of next 2 FPdc 2 rows **below**; repeat from ★ across to last 3 sc, sc in last 3 sc.

Rows 12-15: Repeat Rows 10 and 11 twice.

Repeat Rows 4-15 for pattern.

Chiseled Columns

Chain a multiple of 8 + 5 chs.

Row 1 (Right side)**:** Dc in fourth ch from hook (**3 skipped chs count as first dc**) and in next ch, ★ skip next 2 chs, 5 dc in next ch, skip next 2 chs, dc in next 3 chs; repeat from ★ across.

Note: Loop a short piece of yarn around any stitch to mark Row 1 as **right** side.

To work Back Post double crochet (abbreviated BPdc), YO, insert hook from **back** to **front** around post of st indicated *(Fig. 1, page 79)*, YO and pull up a loop (3 loops on hook), (YO and draw through 2 loops on hook) twice.

To work Front Post double crochet 5 together (abbreviated FPdc5tog) (uses next 5 dc), ★ YO, insert hook from **front** to **back** around post of **next** dc *(Fig. 1, page 79)*, YO and pull up a loop, YO and draw through 2 loops on hook; repeat from ★ 4 times **more**, YO and draw through all 6 loops on hook (**counts as one decrease**).

Row 2: Ch 3 (**counts as first dc, now and throughout**), turn; work BPdc around each of next 2 dc, ch 2, work FPdc5tog, ch 2, ★ work BPdc around each of next 3 dc, ch 2, work FPdc5tog, ch 2; repeat from ★ across to last 3 dc, work BPdc around each of next 2 dc, dc in last dc.

To work Front Post double crochet (abbreviated FPdc), YO, insert hook from **front** to **back** around post of BPdc indicated *(Fig. 1, page 79)*, YO and pull up a loop (3 loops on hook), (YO and draw through 2 loops on hook) twice.

Row 3: Ch 3, turn; work FPdc around each of next 2 BPdc, 5 dc in next decrease, (work FPdc around each of next 3 BPdc, 5 dc in next decrease) across to last 3 sts, work FPdc around each of next 2 BPdc, dc in last dc.

Row 4: Ch 3, turn; work BPdc around each of next 2 FPdc, ch 2, work FPdc5tog, ch 2, ★ work BPdc around each of next 3 FPdc, ch 2, work FPdc5tog, ch 2; repeat from ★ across to last 3 sts, work BPdc around each of next 2 FPdc, dc in last dc.

Repeat Rows 3 and 4 for pattern.

Large Diamonds

Chain a multiple of 8 + 7 chs.

Row 1 (Right side)**:** Dc in fourth ch from hook (**3 skipped chs count as first dc**) and in each ch across.

Note: Loop a short piece of yarn around any stitch to mark Row 1 as **right** side.

Row 2: Ch 1, turn; sc in each dc across.

To work Front Post double crochet (abbreviated FPdc), YO, working in **front** of previous row *(Fig. 2, page 80)*, insert hook from **front** to **back** around post of st indicated *(Fig. 1, page 79)*, YO and pull up a loop (3 loops on hook), (YO and draw through 2 loops on hook) twice.

Row 3: Ch 3 (**counts as first dc, now and throughout**), turn; dc in next 4 sc, ★ skip next sc, work FPdc around dc one row **below** next sc, skip next sc from last dc made, dc in next sc, work FPdc around same dc as last FPdc, skip next sc from last dc made, dc in next 5 dc; repeat from ★ across.

Row 4: Ch 1, turn; sc in each st across.

Row 5: Ch 3, turn; dc in next 3 sc, work FPdc around next FPdc 2 rows **below**, ★ skip next sc from last dc made, dc in next 3 sc, work FPdc around next FPdc 2 rows **below**; repeat from ★ across to last 5 sc, skip next sc from last dc made, dc in last 4 sc.

Row 6: Ch 1, turn; sc in each st across.

Row 7: Ch 3, turn; dc in next 2 sc, work FPdc around next FPdc 2 rows **below**, skip next sc from last dc made, dc in next 5 sc, work FPdc around next FPdc 2 rows **below**, ★ skip next sc from last dc made, dc in next sc, work FPdc around next FPdc 2 rows **below**, skip next sc from last dc made, dc in next 5 sc, work FPdc around next FPdc 2 rows **below**; repeat from ★ across to last 4 sc, skip next sc from last dc made, dc in last 3 sc.

Row 8: Ch 1, turn; sc in each st across.

Row 9: Ch 3, turn; skip next 2 sc, work FPdc around next FPdc one row **below** next sc, ch 1, working in **front** of last FPdc made, work FPdc around dc one row **below** first skipped sc, ★ skip next 3 sc from last dc made, dc in next 5 sc, skip next 2 sc, work FPdc around st one row **below** next sc, ch 1, working in **front** of last FPdc made, work FPdc around st one row **below** first skipped sc; repeat from ★ across to last 4 sc, skip next 3 sc from last dc made, dc in last dc.

Row 10: Ch 1, turn; sc in each st and in each ch-1 sp across.

Row 11: Ch 3, turn; dc in next 3 sc, skip first FPdc 2 rows **below**, work FPdc around next FPdc, ★ skip next sc from last dc made, dc in next 3 sc, work FPdc around next FPdc 2 rows **below**; repeat from ★ across to last 5 sc, skip next sc from last dc made, dc in last 4 sc.

Row 12: Ch 1, turn; sc in each st across.

Row 13: Ch 3, turn; dc in next 4 sc, ★ work FPdc around next FPdc 2 rows **below**, skip next sc from last dc made, dc in next sc, work FPdc around next FPdc 2 rows **below**, skip next sc from last dc made, dc in next 5 sc; repeat from ★ across.

Row 14: Ch 1, turn; sc in each st across.

Row 15: Ch 3, turn; dc in next 4 dc, ★ skip next FPdc 2 rows **below**, work FPdc around next FPdc, ch 1, working in **front** of last FPdc made, work FPdc around skipped FPdc, skip next 3 sc from last dc made, dc in next 5 sc; repeat from ★ across.

Row 16: Ch 1, turn; sc in each st and in each ch-1 sp across.

Repeat Rows 5-16 for pattern.

Broken Stripes

Note: Uses Colors A, B, and C.

With Color A, chain a multiple of 6 + 5 chs.

Row 1 (Right side)**:** Dc in fourth ch from hook **(3 skipped chs count as first dc)** and in each ch across; finish off.

Note: Loop a short piece of yarn around any stitch to mark Row 1 as **right** side.

Row 2: With **wrong** side facing, join Color B with dc in first dc *(see Joining With Dc, page 79)*; dc in next dc and in each dc across.

To work Front Post double crochet (abbreviated FPdc), YO, insert hook from **front** to **back** around post of dc indicated *(Fig. 1, page 79)*, (YO and draw through 2 loops on hook) twice.

Row 3: Ch 3 **(counts as first dc, now and throughout)**, turn; dc in next 2 dc changing to Color C in last dc made *(Fig. A)*, ★ work FPdc around each of next 3 dc changing to Color B in last FPdc made, dc in next 3 dc changing to Color C in last dc made; repeat from ★ across; cut Color B.

Row 4: Ch 3, turn; dc in next st and in each st across; finish off.

Row 5: With **right** side facing, join Color A with dc in first dc; dc in next dc and in each dc across; finish off.

Repeat Rows 2-5 for pattern.

Fig. A

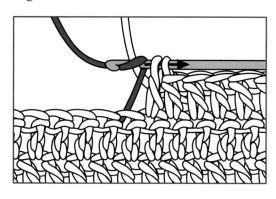

Full Bloom

Chain a multiple of 8 + 10 chs.

Row 1 (Right side): Hdc in third ch from hook **(2 skipped chs count as first hdc)** and in each ch across.

Note: Loop a short piece of yarn around any stitch to mark Row 1 as **right** side.

Row 2: Ch 2 **(counts as first hdc, now and throughout)**, turn; hdc in next hdc and in each hdc across.

To work Front Post treble crochet (abbreviated FPtr), YO twice, working in **front** of previous row *(Fig. 2, page 80)*, insert hook from **front** to **back** around post of hdc indicated *(Fig. 1, page 79)*, YO and pull up a loop (4 loops on hook), (YO and draw through 2 loops on hook) 3 times. Skip hdc behind FPtr.

To work Popcorn (uses one hdc), 5 hdc in hdc indicated, drop loop from hook, insert hook from **front** to **back** in first hdc of 5-hdc group, hook dropped loop and draw through st.

Row 3: Ch 2, turn; hdc in next hdc, skip next 2 hdc, work FPtr around hdc one row **below** next hdc, hdc in next hdc, work Popcorn in next hdc, hdc in next hdc, work FPtr around same hdc as last FPtr made, ★ hdc in next 3 hdc, skip next 2 hdc, work FPtr around hdc one row **below** next hdc, hdc in next hdc, work Popcorn in next hdc, hdc in next hdc, work FPtr around same hdc as last FPtr made; repeat from ★ across to last 2 hdc, hdc in last 2 hdc.

Row 4: Ch 2, turn; hdc in next st and in each st across.

Row 5: Ch 2, turn; hdc in next 5 hdc, skip next 2 hdc, work FPtr around hdc one row **below** next hdc, hdc in next hdc, work Popcorn in next hdc, hdc in next hdc, work FPtr around same hdc as last FPtr made, ★ hdc in next 3 hdc, skip next 2 hdc, work FPtr around hdc one row **below** next hdc, hdc in next hdc, work Popcorn in next hdc, hdc in next hdc, work FPtr around same hdc as last FPtr made; repeat from ★ across to last 6 hdc, hdc in last 6 hdc.

Row 6: Ch 2, turn; hdc in next st and in each st across.

Repeat Rows 3-6 for pattern.

Snug as a Bug

Chain a multiple of 12 + 2 chs.

Row 1 (Right side)**:** Sc in second ch from hook, ★ ch 3, skip next 2 chs, dc in next 3 chs, ch 3, skip next ch, dc in next 3 chs, ch 3, skip next 2 chs, sc in next ch; repeat from ★ across.

Note: Loop a short piece of yarn around any stitch to mark Row 1 as **right** side.

To work Back Post double crochet (abbreviated BPdc), YO, insert hook from **back** to **front** around post of st indicated *(Fig. 1, page 79)*, YO and pull up a loop (3 loops on hook), (YO and draw through 2 loops on hook) twice.

Row 2: Ch 4 (**counts as first dc plus ch 1, now and throughout**), turn; work BPdc around each of next 3 dc, ch 3, sc in next ch-3 sp, ch 3, work BPdc around each of next 3 dc, ★ ch 3, skip next 2 ch-3 sps, work BPdc around each of next 3 dc, ch 3, sc in next ch-3 sp, ch 3, work BPdc around each of next 3 dc; repeat from ★ across to last sc, ch 1, dc in last sc.

To work Front Post double crochet (abbreviated FPdc), YO, insert hook from **front** to **back** around post of st indicated *(Fig. 1, page 79)*, YO and pull up a loop (3 loops on hook), (YO and draw through 2 loops on hook) twice.

To work Cluster (uses one st or sp), ★ YO, insert hook in st or sp indicated, YO and pull up a loop, YO and draw through 2 loops on hook; repeat from ★ 2 times **more**, YO and draw through all 4 loops on hook.

Row 3: Ch 3 (**counts as first dc, now and throughout**), turn; work FPdc around each of next 3 BPdc, ch 2, work (Cluster, ch 2) twice in next sc, work FPdc around each of next 3 BPdc, ★ skip next ch-3 sp, work FPdc around each of next 3 BPdc, ch 2, work (Cluster, ch 2) twice in next sc, work FPdc around each of next 3 BPdc; repeat from ★ across to last dc, dc in last dc.

Row 4: Ch 3, turn; work BPdc around each of next 3 FPdc, ch 2, skip next ch-2 sp, work (Cluster, ch 2) twice in next ch-2 sp, skip next ch-2 sp, ★ work BPdc around each of next 6 FPdc, ch 2, skip next ch-2 sp, work (Cluster, ch 2) twice in next ch-2 sp, skip next ch-2 sp; repeat from ★ across to last 4 sts, work BPdc around each of next 3 FPdc, dc in last dc.

Row 5: Ch 3, turn; work FPdc around each of next 3 BPdc, ch 2, skip next ch-2 sp, work (Cluster, ch 2) twice in next ch-2 sp, skip next ch-2 sp, ★ work FPdc around each of next 6 BPdc, ch 2, skip next ch-2 sp, work (Cluster, ch 2) twice in next ch-2 sp, skip next ch-2 sp; repeat from ★ across to last 4 sts, work FPdc around each of next 3 BPdc, dc in last dc.

Row 6: Ch 3, turn; work BPdc around each of next 3 FPdc, ch 2, skip next ch-2 sp, work (Cluster, ch 2) twice in next ch-2 sp, skip next ch-2 sp, ★ work BPdc around each of next 6 FPdc, ch 2, skip next ch-2 sp, work (Cluster, ch 2) twice in next ch-2 sp, skip next ch-2 sp; repeat from ★ across to last 4 sts, work BPdc around each of next 3 FPdc, dc in last dc.

Row 7: Ch 3, turn; work FPdc around each of next 3 BPdc, ch 3, skip next ch-2 sp, sc in next ch-2 sp, ch 3, skip next ch-2 sp, work FPdc around each of next 3 BPdc, ★ ch 3, FPdc around each of next 3 BPdc, ch 3, skip next ch-2 sp, sc in next ch-2 sp, ch 3, skip next ch-2 sp, work FPdc around each of next 3 BPdc; repeat from ★ across to last dc, dc in last dc.

Row 8: Ch 4, turn; work BPdc around each of next 3 FPdc, ch 3, skip next 2 ch-3 sps, work BPdc around each of next 3 FPdc, ★ ch 3, sc in next ch-3 sp, ch 3, work BPdc around each of next 3 FPdc, ch 3, skip next 2 ch-3 sps, work BPdc around each of next 3 FPdc; repeat from ★ across to last dc, ch 1, dc in last dc.

Row 9: Ch 3, turn; work Cluster in first dc, ch 2, work FPdc around each of next 3 BPdc, skip next ch-3 sp, work FPdc around each of next 3 BPdc, ch 2, ★ work (Cluster, ch 2) twice in next sc, work FPdc around each of next 3 BPdc, skip next ch-3 sp, work FPdc around each of next 3 BPdc, ch 2; repeat from ★ across to last dc, work (Cluster, dc) in last dc.

Row 10: Ch 3, turn; work Cluster in first dc, ch 2, skip next ch-2 sp, work BPdc around each of next 6 FPdc, ch 2, skip next ch-2 sp, ★ work (Cluster, ch 2) twice in next ch-2 sp, skip next ch-2 sp, work BPdc around each of next 6 FPdc, ch 2, skip next ch-2 sp; repeat from ★ across to last 2 sts, skip next Cluster, work (Cluster, dc) in last dc.

Row 11: Ch 3, turn; work Cluster in first dc, ch 2, skip next ch-2 sp, work FPdc around each of next 6 BPdc, ch 2, skip next ch-2 sp, ★ work (Cluster, ch 2) twice in next ch-2 sp, skip next ch-2 sp, work FPdc around each of next 6 BPdc, ch 2, skip next ch-2 sp; repeat from ★ across to last 2 sts, skip next Cluster, work (Cluster, dc) in last dc.

Row 12: Ch 3, turn; work Cluster in first dc, ch 2, skip next ch-2 sp, work BPdc around each of next 6 FPdc, ch 2, skip next ch-2 sp, ★ work (Cluster, ch 2) twice in next ch-2 sp, skip next ch-2 sp, work BPdc around each of next 6 FPdc, ch 2, skip next ch-2 sp; repeat from ★ across to last 2 sts, skip next Cluster, work (Cluster, dc) in last dc.

Row 13: Ch 1, turn; sc in first dc, ch 3, skip next ch-2 sp, work FPdc around each of next 3 BPdc, ch 3, work FPdc around each of next 3 BPdc, ch 3, skip next ch-2 sp, ★ sc in next ch-2 sp, ch 3, skip next ch-2 sp, work FPdc around each of next 3 BPdc, ch 3, work FPdc around each of next 3 BPdc, ch 3, skip next ch-2 sp; repeat from ★ across to last 2 sts, skip next Cluster, sc in last dc.

Row 14: Ch 4, turn; work BPdc around each of next 3 FPdc, ch 3, sc in next ch-3 sp, ch 3, work BPdc around each of next 3 FPdc, ★ ch 3, skip next 2 ch-3 sps, work BPdc around each of next 3 FPdc, ch 3, sc in next ch-3 sp, ch 3, work BPdc around each of next 3 FPdc; repeat from ★ across to last sc, ch 1, dc in last sc.

Repeat Rows 3-14 for pattern.

Bricks

Note: Uses MC and CC in the following sequence: 1 Row MC, ★ 2 rows **each** CC, MC; repeat from ★ for stripe sequence.

With MC, chain a multiple of 4 + 5 chs.

Row 1 (Wrong side): Dc in fourth ch from hook **(3 skipped chs count as first dc)** and in each ch across; finish off.

Note: Loop a short piece of yarn around the **back** of any stitch on Row 1 to mark **right** side.

Row 2: With **right** side facing, join CC with sc in first dc *(see Joining With Sc, page 79)*; sc in next dc and in each dc across.

Row 3: Ch 1, turn; sc in each sc across; finish off.

To work Front Post double crochet (abbreviated FPdc), YO, working in **front** of previous rows *(Fig. 2, page 80)*, insert hook from **front** to **back** around post of dc indicated *(Fig. 1, page 79)*, YO and pull up a loop (3 loops on hook), (YO and draw through 2 loops on hook) twice. Skip sc behind FPdc.

Row 4: With **right** side facing, join MC with sc in first sc; sc in next 2 sc, ★ work FPdc around dc 2 rows **below** next sc, sc in next 3 sc; repeat from ★ across.

Row 5: Ch 3 **(counts as first dc, now and throughout)**, turn; dc in next st and in each st across; finish off.

Row 6: With **right** side facing, join CC with sc in first dc; sc in next dc and in each dc across.

Row 7: Ch 1, turn; sc in each sc across; finish off.

Row 8: With **right** side facing, join MC with sc in first sc; work FPdc around dc 2 rows **below** next sc, ★ sc in next 3 sc, work FPdc around dc 2 rows **below** next sc; repeat from ★ across to last sc, sc in last sc.

Row 9: Ch 3, turn; dc in next st and in each st across; finish off.

Row 10: With **right** side facing, join CC with sc in first dc; sc in next dc and in each dc across.

Row 11: Ch 1, turn; sc in each sc across; finish off.

Repeat Rows 4-11 for pattern.

Boxed Clusters

Chain a multiple of 6 + 2 chs.

Row 1 (Right side): Dc in third ch from hook, ch 2, skip next ch, dc in next ch, ch 2, ★ skip next ch, (YO, insert hook in **next** ch, YO and pull up a loop, YO and draw through 2 loops on hook) 3 times, YO and draw through all 4 loops on hook, ch 2, skip next ch, dc in next ch, ch 2; repeat from ★ across to last 3 chs, skip next ch, (YO, insert hook in **next** ch, YO and pull up a loop, YO and draw through 2 loops on hook) twice, YO and draw through all 3 loops on hook.

Note: Loop a short piece of yarn around any stitch to mark Row 1 as **right** side.

Row 2: Ch 1, turn; sc in first st, ★ ch 2, skip next ch-2 sp, sc in next st; repeat from ★ across.

To work Front Post double crochet (abbreviated FPdc), YO, insert hook from **front** to **back** around post of sc indicated *(Fig. 1, page 79)*, YO and pull up a loop (3 loops on hook), (YO and draw through 2 loops on hook) twice.

To work Front Post double crochet Cluster (abbreviated FPdc Cluster) (uses 2 ch-2 sps and one sc), † YO, insert hook in **next** ch-2 sp, YO and pull up a loop, YO and draw through 2 loops on hook †, YO, insert hook from **front** to **back** around post of next sc *(Fig. 1, page 79)*, YO and pull up a loop, YO and draw through 2 loops on hook, repeat from † to † once, YO and draw through all 4 loops on hook.

To decrease (uses last ch-2 sp and last sc), YO, insert hook in last ch-2 sp, YO and pull up a loop, YO and draw through 2 loops on hook, YO, insert hook in last sc, YO and pull up a loop, YO and draw through 2 loops on hook, YO and draw through all 3 loops on hook.

Row 3: Ch 2, turn; dc in next ch-2 sp, ch 2, work FPdc around next sc, ch 2, ★ work FPdc Cluster, ch 2, work FPdc around next sc, ch 2; repeat from ★ across to last ch-2 sp, decrease.

Row 4: Ch 1, turn; sc in first st, ★ ch 2, skip next ch-2 sp, sc in next st; repeat from ★ across.

Repeat Rows 3 and 4 for pattern.

Shell Spires

Chain a multiple of 10 + 3 chs.

Row 1 (Wrong side)**:** Dc in fourth ch from hook (**3 skipped chs count as first dc**) and in each ch across.

Note: Loop a short piece of yarn around the **back** of any stitch on Row 1 to mark **right** side.

Row 2: Ch 3 (**counts as first dc, now and throughout**), turn; dc in next 2 dc, skip next 2 dc, 5 dc in next dc, ★ skip next 2 dc, dc in next 5 dc, skip next 2 dc, 5 dc in next dc; repeat from ★ across to last 5 dc, skip next 2 dc, dc in last 3 dc.

Row 3: Ch 3, turn; dc in next dc and in each dc across.

To work Split Front Post treble crochet (abbreviated Split FPtr), YO twice, working in **front** of previous rows *(Fig. 2, page 80)*, insert hook from **front** to **back** around post of dc **before** 5-dc group 2 rows **below** *(Fig. 1, page 79)*, YO and pull up a loop (4 loops on hook), (YO and draw through 2 loops on hook) twice, YO twice, insert hook from **front** to **back** around post of dc **after** same 5-dc group, YO and pull up a loop (5 loops on hook), (YO and draw through 2 loops on hook) twice, YO and draw through all 3 loops on hook. Skip dc behind Split FPtr.

Row 4: Ch 3, turn; dc in next 4 dc, work Split FPtr, ch 3, slip st in top of st just made, ★ dc in next 9 dc, work Split FPtr, ch 3, slip st in top of st just made; repeat from ★ across to last 5 dc, dc in last 5 dc.

To treble crochet (abbreviated tr), YO twice, working in **front** of previous row *(Fig. 2, page 80)*, insert hook in dc indicated, YO and pull up a loop (4 loops on hook), (YO and draw through 2 loops on hook) 3 times.

Row 5: Ch 3, turn; dc in next 4 dc, tr in skipped dc one row **below**, (dc in next 9 dc, tr in skipped dc one row **below**) across to last 5 dc, dc in last 5 dc.

Rows 6 and 7: Ch 3, turn; dc in next st and in each st across.

Repeat Rows 2-7 for pattern.

Interruption

Note: Uses Colors A, B, and C in the following sequence: ★ 2 Rows **each** Color A, Color B, Color C; repeat from ★ for stripe sequence.

With Color A, chain a multiple of 6 + 4 chs.

Row 1 (Right side)**:** Sc in second ch from hook and in each ch across.

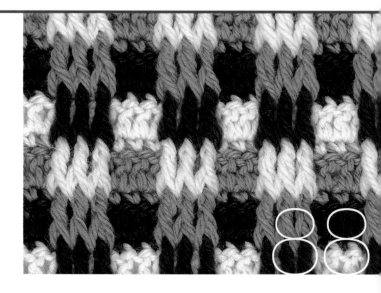

Note: Loop a short piece of yarn around any stitch to mark Row 1 as **right** side.

Row 2: Ch 3 (**counts as first dc, now and throughout**), turn; dc in next sc and in each sc across; finish off.

To work Front Post double crochet (abbreviated FPdc), YO, working in **front** of previous row (**Fig. 2, page 80**), insert hook from **front** to **back** around post of st indicated (**Fig. 1, page 79**), YO and pull up a loop (3 loops on hook), (YO and draw through 2 loops on hook) twice. Skip dc behind FPdc.

Row 3: With **right** side facing, join Color B with sc in first dc (*see Joining With Sc, page 79*); sc in next 2 dc, ★ work FPdc around sc one row **below** each of next 3 dc, sc in next 3 dc; repeat from ★ across.

Row 4: Ch 3, turn; dc in next st and in each st across; finish off.

Row 5: With **right** side facing, join Color C with sc in first dc; sc in next 2 dc, ★ work FPdc around FPdc one row **below** each of next 3 dc, sc in next 3 dc; repeat from ★ across.

Repeat Rows 4 and 5 for pattern, working in stripe sequence.

Stand-Out Posts

Chain a multiple of 6 + 9 chs.

Row 1 (Wrong side): Dc in fourth ch from hook (**3 skipped chs count as first dc**) and in next 4 chs, ch 1, ★ skip next ch, dc in next 5 chs, ch 1; repeat from ★ across to last 7 chs, skip next ch, dc in last 6 chs.

Note: Loop a short piece of yarn around the **back** of any stitch on Row 1 to mark **right** side.

To work Front Post double crochet (abbreviated FPdc), YO, insert hook from **front** to **back** around post of st indicated (**Fig. 1, page 79**), YO and pull up a loop (3 loops on hook), (YO and draw through 2 loops on hook) twice.

Row 2: Ch 3 (**counts as first dc, now and throughout**), turn; dc in next 2 dc, work FPdc around next dc, ★ dc in next 2 dc, ch 1, dc in next 2 dc, work FPdc around next dc; repeat from ★ across to last 3 dc, dc in last 3 dc.

To work Back Post double crochet (abbreviated BPdc), YO, insert hook from **back** to **front** around post of FPdc indicated (**Fig. 1, page 79**), YO and pull up a loop (3 loops on hook), (YO and draw through 2 loops on hook) twice.

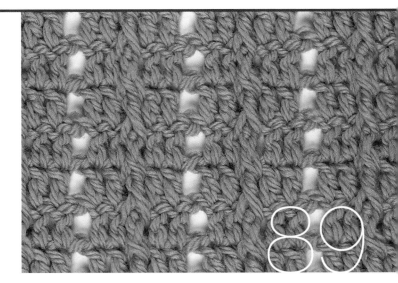

Row 3: Ch 3, turn; dc in next 2 dc, work BPdc around next FPdc, ★ dc in next 2 dc, ch 1, dc in next 2 dc, work BPdc around next FPdc; repeat from ★ across to last 3 dc, dc in last 3 dc.

Row 4: Ch 3, turn; dc in next 2 dc, work FPdc around next BPdc, ★ dc in next 2 dc, ch 1, dc in next 2 dc, work FPdc around next BPdc; repeat from ★ across to last 3 dc, dc in last 3 dc.

Repeat Rows 3 and 4 for pattern.

Open Chevron

Chain a multiple of 4 + 2 chs.

Row 1 (Right side)**:** Hdc in third ch from hook (**2 skipped chs count as first hdc**) and in each ch across.

Note: Loop a short piece of yarn around any stitch to mark Row 1 as **right** side.

Row 2: Ch **2** (**counts as first hdc, now and throughout**), turn; hdc in next hdc and in each hdc across.

To work Front Post treble crochet (abbreviated FPtr), YO twice, insert hook from **front** to **back** around post of hdc indicated *(Fig. 1, page 79)*, YO and pull up a loop (4 loops on hook), (YO and draw through 2 loops on hook) 3 times.

Row 3: Ch 3 (**counts as first dc, now and throughout**), turn; skip next hdc, dc in next 2 hdc, working in **front** of last 2 dc made, work FPtr around skipped hdc, ★ ch 1, skip next 2 hdc, dc in next 2 hdc, working in **front** of last 2 dc made, work FPtr around second skipped hdc; repeat from ★ across to last hdc, dc in last hdc.

To work Back Post treble crochet (abbreviated BPtr), YO twice, insert hook from **back** to **front** around post of FPtr indicated *(Fig. 1, page 79)*, YO and pull up a loop (4 loops on hook), (YO and draw through 2 loops on hook) 3 times.

Row 4: Ch 3, turn; skip next FPtr, dc in next 2 dc, working **behind** last 2 dc made, work BPtr around skipped FPtr, ★ ch 1, skip next FPtr, dc in next 2 dc, working **behind** last 2 dc made, work BPtr around skipped FPtr; repeat from ★ across to last dc, dc in last dc.

Row 5: Ch 2, turn; hdc in next st and in each st and ch-1 sp across.

Row 6: Ch 2, turn; hdc in next hdc and in each hdc across.

Row 7: Ch 3, turn; skip next hdc, dc in next 2 hdc, working in **front** of last 2 dc made, work FPtr around skipped hdc, ★ ch 1, skip next 2 hdc, dc in next 2 hdc, working in **front** of last 2 dc made, work FPtr around second skipped hdc; repeat from ★ across to last hdc, dc in last hdc.

Repeat Rows 4-7 for pattern.

Regal

Chain a multiple of 10 + 3 chs.

Row 1 (Wrong side)**:** 2 Dc in sixth ch from hook **(5 skipped chs count as first dc and 2 skipped chs)**, ch 1, dc in next 3 chs, ch 1, 2 dc in next ch, skip next 2 chs, dc in next ch, ★ skip next 2 chs, 2 dc in next ch, ch 1, dc in next 3 chs, ch 1, 2 dc in next ch, skip next 2 chs, dc in next ch; repeat from ★ across.

Note: Loop a short piece of yarn around the **back** of any stitch on Row 1 to mark **right** side.

To work Front Post double crochet *(abbreviated FPdc)*, YO, insert hook from **front** to **back** around post of st indicated *(Fig. 1, page 79)*, YO and pull up a loop (3 loops on hook), (YO and draw through 2 loops on hook) twice.

Row 2: Ch 3 **(counts as first dc, now and throughout)**, turn; 2 dc in next ch-1 sp, ch 1, work FPdc around each of next 3 dc, ch 1, 2 dc in next ch-1 sp, ★ skip next 2 dc, work FPdc around next dc, 2 dc in next ch-1 sp, ch 1, work FPdc around each of next 3 dc, ch 1, 2 dc in next ch-1 sp; repeat from ★ across to last 3 dc, skip next 2 dc, dc in last dc.

To work Back Post double crochet *(abbreviated BPdc)*, YO, insert hook from **back** to **front** around post of FPdc indicated *(Fig. 1, page 79)*, YO and pull up a loop (3 loops on hook), (YO and draw through 2 loops on hook) twice.

Row 3: Ch 3, turn; 2 dc in next ch-1 sp, ch 1, work BPdc around each of next 3 FPdc, ch 1, 2 dc in next ch-1 sp, ★ skip next 2 dc, work BPdc around next FPdc, 2 dc in next ch-1 sp, ch 1, work BPdc around each of next 3 FPdc, ch 1, 2 dc in next ch-1 sp; repeat from ★ across to last 3 dc, skip next 2 dc, dc in last dc.

Row 4: Ch 3, turn; 2 dc in next ch-1 sp, ch 1, work FPdc around each of next 3 BPdc, ch 1, 2 dc in next ch-1 sp, ★ skip next 2 dc, work FPdc around next BPdc, 2 dc in next ch-1 sp, ch 1, work FPdc around each of next 3 BPdc, ch 1, 2 dc in next ch-1 sp; repeat from ★ across to last 3 dc, skip next 2 dc, dc in last dc.

Repeat Rows 3 and 4 for pattern.

Cable & Shell Duo

Chain a multiple of 7 + 6 chs.

Row 1 (Wrong side)**:** Dc in fourth ch from hook **(3 skipped chs count as first dc)** and in next ch, skip next 2 chs, (2 dc, ch 1, 2 dc) in next ch, ★ skip next 2 chs, dc in next 2 chs, skip next 2 chs, (2 dc, ch 1, 2 dc) in next ch; repeat from ★ across to last 5 chs, skip next 2 chs, dc in last 3 chs.

Note: Loop a short piece of yarn around the **back** of any stitch on Row 1 to mark **right** side.

To work Front Post double crochet (abbreviated FPdc), YO, insert hook from **front** to **back** around post of st indicated *(Fig. 1, page 79)*, YO and pull up a loop (3 loops on hook), (YO and draw through 2 loops on hook) twice.

Row 2: Ch 3 **(counts as first dc, now and throughout),** turn; skip next dc, work FPdc around next dc, working in **front** of FPdc just made, work FPdc around skipped dc, ★ (2 dc, ch 1, 2 dc) in next ch-1 sp, skip next 3 dc, work FPdc around next dc, working in **front** of FPdc just made, work FPdc around third skipped dc; repeat from ★ across to last dc, dc in last dc.

To work Back Post double crochet (abbreviated BPdc), YO, insert hook from **back** to **front** around post of FPdc indicated *(Fig. 1, page 79)*, YO and pull up a loop (3 loops on hook), (YO and draw through 2 loops on hook) twice.

Row 3: Ch 3, turn; work BPdc around each of next 2 FPdc, ★ (2 dc, ch 1, 2 dc) in next ch-1 sp, skip next 2 dc, work BPdc around each of next 2 FPdc; repeat from ★ across to last dc, dc in last dc.

Row 4: Ch 3, turn; skip next BPdc, work FPdc around next BPdc, working in **front** of FPdc just made, work FPdc around skipped BPdc, ★ (2 dc, ch 1, 2 dc) in next ch-1 sp, skip next 3 sts, work FPdc around next BPdc, working in **front** of FPdc just made, work FPdc around third skipped st; repeat from ★ across to last dc, dc in last dc.

Repeat Rows 3 and 4 for pattern.

Lace Bands

Chain a multiple of 12 + 7 chs.

Row 1 (Right side)**:** Dc in fourth ch from hook **(3 skipped chs count as first dc)** and in next 2 chs, skip next ch, (dc, ch 1, dc) in next ch, [skip next 2 chs, (dc, ch 1, dc) in next ch] twice, ★ skip next ch, dc in next 3 chs, skip next ch, (dc, ch 1, dc) in next ch, [skip next 2 chs, (dc, ch 1, dc) in next ch] twice; repeat from ★ across to last 5 chs, skip next ch, dc in last 4 chs.

Note: Loop a short piece of yarn around any stitch to mark Row 1 as **right** side.

To work Back Post double crochet (abbreviated BPdc), YO, insert hook from **back** to **front** around post of st indicated *(Fig. 1, page 79)*, YO and pull up a loop (3 loops on hook), (YO and draw through 2 loops on hook) twice.

Row 2: Ch 3 **(counts as first dc, now and throughout),** turn; work BPdc around each of next 3 dc, ★ (dc, ch 1, dc) in each of next 3 ch-1 sps, skip next dc, work BPdc around each of next 3 dc; repeat from ★ across to last dc, dc in last dc.

To work Front Post double crochet (abbreviated FPdc), YO, insert hook from **front** to **back** around post of BPdc indicated *(Fig. 1, page 79)*, YO and pull up a loop (3 loops on hook), (YO and draw through 2 loops on hook) twice.

Row 3: Ch 3, turn; work FPdc around each of next 3 BPdc, ★ (dc, ch 1, dc) in each of next 3 ch-1 sps, skip next dc, work FPdc around each of next 3 BPdc; repeat from ★ across to last dc, dc in last dc.

Row 4: Ch 3, turn; work BPdc around each of next 3 FPdc, ★ (dc, ch 1, dc) in each of next 3 ch-1 sps, skip next dc, work BPdc around each of next 3 FPdc; repeat from ★ across to last dc, dc in last dc.

Repeat Rows 3 and 4 for pattern.

Bobbled Rib

Chain a multiple of 4 + 2 chs.

Row 1 (Right side)**:** Sc in second ch from hook and in each ch across.

Note: Loop a short piece of yarn around any stitch to mark Row 1 as **right** side.

Row 2: Ch 1, turn; sc in each sc across.

To work Front Post double crochet *(abbreviated FPdc)*, YO, working in **front** of previous row *(Fig. 2, page 80)*, insert hook from **front** to **back** around post of st indicated *(Fig. 1, page 79)*, YO and pull up a loop (3 loops on hook), (YO and draw through 2 loops on hook) twice. Skip sc behind FPdc.

Row 3: Ch 1, turn; sc in first sc, work FPdc around sc one row **below** each of next 3 sc, ★ 5 sc in next sc, work FPdc around sc one row **below** each of next 3 sc; repeat from ★ across to last sc, sc in last sc.

Row 4: Ch 1, turn; sc in first 4 sts, pull up a loop in each of next 5 sc, YO and draw through all 6 loops on hook, ★ sc in next 3 FPdc, pull up a loop in each of next 5 sc, YO and draw through all 6 loops on hook; repeat from ★ across to last 4 sts, sc in last 4 sts.

Row 5: Ch 1, turn; sc in first sc, ★ work FPdc around FPdc one row **below** each of next 3 sc, sc in next st; repeat from ★ across.

Row 6: Ch 1, turn; sc in each st across.

Row 7: Ch 1, turn; sc in first sc, work FPdc around FPdc one row **below** each of next 3 sc, ★ 5 sc in next sc, work FPdc around FPdc one row **below** each of next 3 sc; repeat from ★ across to last sc, sc in last sc.

Repeat Rows 4-7 for pattern.

Spaced Dips

Note: Uses Colors A, B, and C in the following sequence: ★ 2 Rows **each** Color A, Color B, Color C; repeat from ★ for stripe sequence.

With Color A, chain a multiple of 4 + 7 chs.

Row 1 (Right side)**:** Dc in fourth ch from hook (**3 skipped chs count as first dc**) and in each ch across.

Note: Loop a short piece of yarn around any stitch to mark Row 1 as **right** side.

Row 2: Ch 1, turn; sc in each dc across; finish off.

To work Front Post double crochet *(abbreviated FPdc)*, YO, working in **front** of previous row *(Fig. 2, page 80)*, insert hook from **front** to **back** around post of dc indicated *(Fig. 1, page 79)*, YO and pull up a loop (3 loops on hook), (YO and draw through 2 loops on hook) twice. Skip sc behind FPdc.

Row 3: With **right** side facing, join Color B with dc in first sc *(see Joining With Dc, page 79)*; dc in next sc, work FPdc around dc one row **below** next sc, ★ dc in next 3 sc, work FPdc around dc one row **below** next sc; repeat from ★ across to last 2 sc, dc in last 2 sc.

Row 4: Ch 1, turn; sc in each st across; finish off.

Row 5: With **right** side facing, join Color C with dc in first sc; ★ dc in next 3 sc, work FPdc around dc one row **below** next sc; repeat from ★ across to last 4 sc, dc in last 4 sc.

Row 6: Ch 1, turn; sc in each st across; finish off.

Repeat Rows 3-6 for pattern, working in stripe sequence.

Vertical Chevrons

Chain a multiple of 8 + 4 chs.

Row 1 (Right side)**:** Hdc in third ch from hook **(2 skipped chs count as first hdc)** and in each ch across.

Note: Loop a short piece of yarn around any stitch to mark Row 1 as **right** side.

Row 2: Ch 2 **(counts as first hdc, now and throughout),** turn; hdc in next hdc and in each hdc across.

To work Front Post double crochet (abbreviated FPdc), YO, working in **front** of previous row *(Fig. 2, page 80),* insert hook from **front** to **back** around post of st indicated *(Fig. 1, page 79),* YO and pull up a loop (3 loops on hook), (YO and draw through 2 loops on hook) twice. Skip hdc behind FPdc.

Row 3: Ch 2, turn; work FPdc around hdc one row **below** next hdc, ★ hdc in next 7 hdc, work FPdc around hdc one row **below** next hdc; repeat from ★ across to last hdc, hdc in last hdc.

Row 4: Ch 2, turn; hdc in next st and in each st across.

To work Front Post double treble crochet (abbreviated FPdtr), YO 3 times, working in **front** of previous row *(Fig. 2, page 80),* insert hook from **front** to **back** around post of hdc indicated *(Fig. 1, page 79),* YO and pull up a loop (5 loops on hook), (YO and draw through 2 loops on hook) 4 times. Skip hdc behind FPdtr.

Row 5: Ch 2, turn; work FPdc around FPdc one row **below** next hdc, hdc in next hdc, ★ skip next 2 hdc, work FPdtr around hdc 3 rows **below** next hdc, hdc in next 3 hdc, work FPdtr around same hdc as last FPdtr made, hdc in next hdc, work FPdc around FPdc one row **below** next hdc, hdc in next hdc; repeat from ★ across.

Row 6: Ch 2, turn; hdc in next st and in each st across.

Repeat Rows 5 and 6 for pattern.

Chisel Stitch

Chain a multiple of 4 + 5 chs.

Row 1 (Wrong side): Dc in fourth ch from hook (**3 skipped chs count as first dc**) and in each ch across.

Note: Loop a short piece of yarn around the **back** of any stitch on Row 1 to mark **right** side.

To work Front Post double crochet (abbreviated FPdc), YO, insert hook from **front** to **back** around post of st indicated *(Fig. 1, page 79)*, YO and pull up a loop (3 loops on hook), (YO and draw through 2 loops on hook) twice.

Row 2: Ch 3 (**counts as first dc, now and throughout**), turn; work FPdc around next dc, (dc in next 3 dc, work FPdc around next dc) across to last dc, dc in last dc.

To work Back Post double crochet (abbreviated BPdc), YO, insert hook from **back** to **front** around post of FPdc indicated *(Fig. 1, page 79)*, YO and pull up a loop (3 loops on hook), (YO and draw through 2 loops on hook) twice.

Row 3: Ch 3, turn; work BPdc around next FPdc, (work FPdc around each of next 3 dc, work BPdc around next FPdc) across to last dc, dc in last dc.

Row 4: Ch 3, turn; dc in next 2 sts, (work FPdc around next BPdc, dc in next 3 sts) across.

Row 5: Ch 3, turn; work FPdc around each of next 2 dc, work BPdc around next FPdc, (work FPdc around each of next 3 dc, work BPdc around next FPdc) across to last 3 dc, work FPdc around each of next 2 dc, dc in last dc.

Row 6: Ch 3, turn; work FPdc around next FPdc, (dc in next 3 sts, work FPdc around next FPdc) across to last dc, dc in last dc.

Repeat Rows 3-6 for pattern.

Posted Shells In A Row

Chain a multiple of 6 + 9 chs.

Row 1 (Wrong side)**:** (2 Dc, ch 1, 2 dc) in sixth ch from hook (**5 skipped chs count as first dc and 2 skipped chs**), skip next 2 chs, dc in next ch, ★ skip next 2 chs, (2 dc, ch 1, 2 dc) in next ch, skip next 2 chs, dc in next ch; repeat from ★ across.

Note: Loop a short piece of yarn around the **back** of any stitch on Row 1 to mark **right** side.

To work Front Post double crochet (*abbreviated FPdc*), YO, insert hook from **front** to **back** around post of st indicated (*Fig. 1, page 79*), YO and pull up a loop (3 loops on hook), (YO and draw through 2 loops on hook) twice.

Row 2: Ch 3 (**counts as first dc, now and throughout**), turn; (2 dc, ch 1, 2 dc) in next ch-1 sp, ★ skip next 2 dc, work FPdc around next dc, (2 dc, ch 1, 2 dc) in next ch-1 sp; repeat from ★ across to last 3 dc, skip next 2 dc, dc in last dc.

To work Back Post double crochet (*abbreviated BPdc*), YO, insert hook from **back** to **front** around post of FPdc indicated (*Fig. 1, page 79*), YO and pull up a loop (3 loops on hook), (YO and draw through 2 loops on hook) twice.

Row 3: Ch 3, turn; (2 dc, ch 1, 2 dc) in next ch-1 sp, ★ skip next 2 dc, work BPdc around next FPdc, (2 dc, ch 1, 2 dc) in next ch-1 sp; repeat from ★ across to last 3 dc, skip next 2 dc, dc in last dc.

Row 4: Ch 3, turn; (2 dc, ch 1, 2 dc) in next ch-1 sp, ★ skip next 2 dc, work FPdc around next BPdc, (2 dc, ch 1, 2 dc) in next ch-1 sp; repeat from ★ across to last 3 dc, skip next 2 dc, dc in last dc.

Repeat Rows 3 and 4 for pattern.

It's A Wrap

Chain a multiple of 6 + 4 chs.

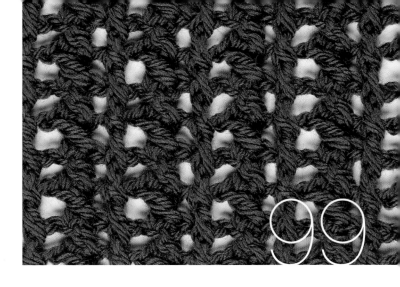

Row 1 (Right side): Dc in eighth ch from hook, ch 1, working in **front** of dc just made, dc in sixth skipped ch (**5 remaining skipped chs count as first dc plus ch 1 and 1 skipped ch**), ch 1, skip next ch, dc in next ch, ★ ch 1, skip next 3 chs, dc in next ch, ch 1, working in **front** of dc just made, dc in second skipped ch, ch 1, skip next ch, dc in next ch; repeat from ★ across.

Note: Loop a short piece of yarn around any stitch to mark Row 1 as **right** side.

To work Back Post double crochet (abbreviated BPdc), YO, insert hook from **back** to **front** around post of st indicated *(Fig. 1, page 79)*, YO and pull up a loop (3 loops on hook), (YO and draw through 2 loops on hook) twice.

Row 2: Ch 4 (**counts as first dc plus ch 1, now and throughout**), turn; skip next dc, dc in next dc, ch 1, working in **front** of dc just made, dc in skipped dc, ch 1, ★ work BPdc around next dc, ch 1, skip next dc, dc in next dc, ch 1, working in **front** of dc just made, dc in skipped dc, ch 1; repeat from ★ across to last dc, dc in last dc.

To work Front Post double crochet (abbreviated FPdc), YO, insert hook from **front** to **back** around post of BPdc indicated *(Fig. 1, page 79)*, YO and pull up a loop (3 loops on hook), (YO and draw through 2 loops on hook) twice.

Row 3: Ch 4, turn; skip next dc, dc in next dc, ch 1, working in **front** of dc just made, dc in skipped dc, ch 1, ★ work FPdc around next BPdc, ch 1, skip next dc, dc in next dc, ch 1, working in **front** of dc just made, dc in skipped dc, ch 1; repeat from ★ across to last dc, dc in last dc.

Row 4: Ch 4, turn; skip next dc, dc in next dc, ch 1, working in **front** of dc just made, dc in skipped dc, ch 1, ★ work BPdc around next FPdc, ch 1, skip next dc, dc in next dc, ch 1, working in **front** of dc just made, dc in skipped dc, ch 1; repeat from ★ across to last dc, dc in last dc.

Repeat Rows 3 and 4 for pattern.

General Instructions

ABBREVIATIONS

BPdc	Back Post double crochet(s)
BPdc2tog	Back Post double crochet 2 together
BPdc3tog	Back Post double crochet 3 together
BPdc5tog	Back Post double crochet 5 together
BPtr	Back Post treble crochet(s)
CC	Contrasting Color
ch(s)	chain(s)
cm	centimeters
dc	double crochet(s)
dc5tog	double crochet 5 together
FP	Front Post
FPdc	Front Post double crochet(s)
FPdc2tog	Front Post double crochet 2 together
FPdc3tog	Front Post double crochet 3 together
FPdc4tog	Front Post double crochet 4 together
FPdc5tog	Front Post double crochet 5 together
FPdc10tog	Front Post double crochet 10 together
FPdtr	Front Post double treble crochet(s)
FPhdc	Front Post half double crochet(s)
FPsc	Front Post single crochet(s)
FPtr	Front Post treble crochet(s)
FPtrtr	Front Post triple treble crochet(s)
hdc	half double crochet(s)
MC	Main Color
mm	millimeters
sc	single crochet(s)
sp(s)	space(s)
st(s)	stitch(es)
tr	treble crochet(s)
YO	yarn over

★ — work instructions following ★ as many **more** times as indicated in addition to the first time.

† to † — work all instructions from first † to second † **as many** times as specified.

( ) or [ ] — work enclosed instructions **as many** times as specified by the number immediately following **or** work all enclosed instructions in the stitch or space indicated **or** contains explanatory remarks.

CROCHET TERMINOLOGY	
UNITED STATES	**INTERNATIONAL**
slip stitch (slip st) =	single crochet (sc)
single crochet (sc) =	double crochet (dc)
half double crochet (hdc) =	half treble crochet (htr)
double crochet (dc) =	treble crochet (tr)
treble crochet (tr) =	double treble crochet (dtr)
double treble crochet (dtr) =	triple treble crochet (ttr)
triple treble crochet (tr tr) =	quadruple treble crochet (qtr)
skip =	miss

CROCHET HOOKS	
UNITED STATES	**METRIC (mm)**
B-1	2.25
C-2	2.75
D-3	3.25
E-4	3.5
F-5	3.75
G-6	4
H-8	5
I-9	5.5
J-10	6
K-10 ½	6.5
N	9
P	10
Q	15

PLANNING AN AFGHAN

When planning an afghan, decide what size afghan you'd like to make, then select your favorite yarn and pattern stitch and make a swatch. Measure the width of one repeat in the swatch to determine the number of pattern repeats necessary to make your afghan the desired size.

For example, if you want to use pattern stitch #87 Shell Spires, on page 66, to make an afghan that is 45" (114.5 cm) wide and your pattern repeat measures 3" (7.5 cm), you'll divide 45 by 3 to determine the number of pattern repeats you need for the desired width (45 divided by 3 = 15 pattern repeats). It takes 10 chains to work one repeat so you'll need 150 chains to work 15 pattern repeats (10 x 15 = 150). Then add any additional chains that are necessary to work the first row of the pattern (150 + 3 = 153 chains).

MULTIPLES

Multiples are the number of stitches required to work a pattern. A very simple pattern could be worked by making a chain using just the numbers given at the beginning of the instructions. However, most patterns need twice the number of stitches given in order for all the rows to work. For example, #93 Lace Bands, on page 71, lists a multiple of 12 plus 7 chains. If you chained 19, you will only be able to work the instructions for the stitches before and after a star (★) repeat. But, if you chained 31 (12 x 2 = 24 + 7 chs), you will be able to work across an entire row.

JOINING WITH SC

When instructed to join with a sc, begin with a slip knot on the hook. Insert the hook in the stitch or space indicated, YO and pull up a loop, YO and draw through both loops on hook.

JOINING WITH DC

When instructed to join with a dc, begin with a slip knot on the hook. YO, holding loop on hook, insert hook in stitch or space indicated, YO and pull up a loop (3 loops on hook), (YO and draw through 2 loops on hook) twice.

POST STITCH

Work around the post of the stitch indicated, inserting the hook in the direction of the arrow (*Fig. 1*).

Fig. 1

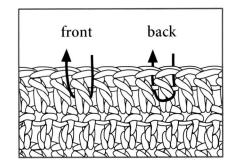

WORKING IN FRONT OF PREVIOUS ROW(S)

Work in stitch or space indicated, inserting the hook in the direction of the arrow (*Fig. 2*).

Fig. 2

WORKING IN A SPACE BEFORE A STITCH

When instructed to work in a space **before** a stitch or in spaces **between** stitches, insert hook in space indicated by arrow (*Fig. 3*).

Fig. 3

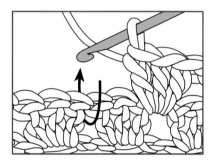

Samples made and instructions tested by Janet Akins.

Production Team: Writer/Technical Editor - Linda Daley; Editorial Writer - Susan McManus Johnson; Senior Graphic Artist - Lora Puls; Graphic Artists - Jacob Casleton and Janie Wright; and Photographer - Ken West.

For digital downloads of Leisure Arts' best-selling designs, visit http://leisureartslibrary.com

We have made every effort to ensure that these instructions are accurate and complete. We cannot, however, be responsible for human error, typographical mistakes, or variations in individual work.